THE DISPOSSESSED
Chronicles of the Desterrados of Colombia

The Dispossessed

CHRONICLES OF THE DESTERRADOS OF COLOMBIA

ALFREDO MOLANO

Translated by Daniel Bland

Foreword by Aviva Chomsky
Introduction by Lance Selfa

Haymarket Books
CHICAGO, ILLINOIS

Originally published as *Desterrados: crónicas del desarraigo*
by El Áncora Editores, Colombia, 2001

This edition published in 2005 by Haymarket Books
P.O.Box 160185, Chicago, IL 60618, USA
www.haymarketbooks.org

ISBN-10: 1-931859-175
ISBN-13: 978-1-931859-17-2

Library of Congress Cataloging-in-Publication data:
Molano, Alfredo.
[Desterrados. English]
The dispossessed : chronicles of the desterrados of Colombia / Alfredo Molano.
p. cm.
Includes bibliographical references.
ISBN 1-931859-17-5 (pbk. : alk. paper)
1. Refugees--Colombia--Case studies. 2. Forced migration--Colombia--Case studies.
3. Refugee children--Colombia--Case studies. 4. Assassination--Colombia--Case
studies. 5. Subversive activities--Colombia--Case studies. 6. Paramilitary forces--
Colombia--Case studies. 7. Social conflict--Colombia--Case studies. I. Title.
HV640.5.C7M6513 2005
986.106'35--dc22
2002021412

Cover design by Ragina Johnson
Interior design and production by Ragina Johnson and David Whitehouse
Printed in Canada
10 9 8 7 6 5 4 3 2 1

A Mónica Restrepo,
cuya risa derrota la muerte.

To Mónica Restrepo, whose
laugh triumphs over death.

Buenos días, memoria terca,
buenos días, sangre seca,
buenos días, hueso acostado.
buenos días, aire sin mano.
(Pensar en hacer burbujas
con el corazón ahogándose).

Jaime Sabines

Table of Contents

Illustrations

Cover photo

Oneida Bocanegra Pulido is eight years old. She was displaced from La Union Peneya, Caquetá. Today, she lives in Florencia, Caquetá, Colombia. *Photograph courtesy Camilo George.*

From Exile

AUC paramilitaries in a jungle camp in southern Colombia, near the town of El Placer, Putamayo, in 2001. *Photograph courtesy Daniel Bland.*

The Defeat

This is Oneida (pictured on the cover), her cousin Margarita, and her grandmother. The three lived together in Union Peneya, in the Caquetá region. On January 4, 2004, with the advance of the army during Operation Patriot, the FARC ordered the 1,500 townspeople to leave the area under penalty of death. Because Margarita was sick with a skin infection, the family could only hide under their beds while the guerrillas searched house to house. When the town was abandoned, the family could leave, but they had neither food nor medicine. The army evacuated the entire family at the end of January to Florencia, Caquetá. *Photograph courtesy Camilo George.*

Ángela

Survivors of the massacre at El Salado, a town of 4,500 inhabitants in the Montes de Maria area. On February 16, 2000, the town experienced one of the most horrific slaughters perpetrated by the paramilitaries who accused the townspeople of aiding the guerrillas. Over three days, 600 paramilitary fighters rounded up all the towns-people that they could take out of the jungle—about 500 people. For four days and nights, the captives were tortured, abused, and killed. One young woman who was gang-raped, had a piece of cactus forced down her throat, causing her to suffocate on her own blood. In the end, the paramilitaries painted anti-guerrilla slogans on houses with the blood of the victims. *Photograph courtesy Camilo George.*

Silences

U.S military-trained and -equipped Colombian army special anti-narcotics commandos on patrol deep in the jungles of Colombia in search of cocaine processing laboratories. *Photograph courtesy Steven Salisbury/Red Dot/Zuma Press.*

The Turkish Boat

Thirteen-year-old Jhonn Nilson lives in the poor neighborhoods of San Jacinto, in Córdoba, where many survivors of the massacres in the Montes de Maria area fled. He looks through trash for nylon sacks so that his grandmother can make backpacks from their threads. They trade the backpacks for food at the San Jacinto market. *Photograph courtesy Camilo George.*

The Garden

Students at a school created by the residents of the La Ceiba neighborhood, in Carmen de Bolivar. This school was founded by a group of neighborhood residents to provide for the increasing number of displaced people that continue to arrive in the neighborhood from the conflict zones of Sucre, Cordoba, and Bolivar. This school has 300 students, but no running water. It is housed in two rooms and the hallway of a house. The students have neither textbooks nor school supplies. The usual breakfast in this school is a soft drink. *Photograph courtesy Camilo George.*

Osiris

Another survivor of the February 2000 El Salado massacre. *Photograph courtesy Camilo George.*

Nubia, La Catira

A relocated girl on a street in Bogotá. Her sign says: "I would like to study; my mother is unemployed; thank you for your help," as she asks drivers for money. *Photograph courtesy Rodrigo Arangua/AFP.*

Colombia

★ Capital city
■ Other city over 200,000
• City under 200,000
⊙ Comunidad de Paz

0   100   200 miles

PANAMA

PACIFIC OCEAN

VENEZUELA

Caracas ★

GUAJIRA
Santa Marta
Barranquilla
ATLÁNTICO
Cartagena
MAGDALENA
CESAR
Curumaní
Pailitas
SUCRE
CÓRDOBA
BOLÍVAR
San José de Apartadó
Tibú
NORTE DE SANTANDER
Cúcuta
Apartadó
Barranca-bermeja
Bucaramanga
Ciudad Sucre
URABÁ
Angostura
SANTANDER
ANTIOQUIA
Caño Limón
Arauca
San Francisco de Asís
Saravena
ARAUCA
CHOCÓ
Medellín
BOYACÁ
Puerto Boyacá
CASANARE
Manizales
VICHADA
Pereira
Cauca
CUNDINAMARCA
Ibagué
TOLIMA
★ Bogotá
Buenaventura
VALLE DEL CAUCA
Cali
Magdalena
GUAVIARE
Neiva
META
GUAINÍA
CAUCA
HUILA
San Vicente del Caguán
NARIÑO
Florencia
Puerto Rico
VAUPÉS
CAQUETÁ
AMAZONAS
ECUADOR
BRAZIL
Putumayo
Amazon
PERU
Amazon

Foreword

By Aviva Chomsky

Most people in the United States know something about Colombia. It's difficult to live in this country and not absorb the idea that Colombia is a dangerous, violent place: a place full of guerrillas, cocaine, and drug traffickers.

Few people in the United States know that Colombia is the third-largest recipient of U.S. military aid in the world; that more journalists, teachers, and trade unionists are killed every year in Colombia than anywhere else in the world; and that the perpetrators of the violence in Colombia are, overwhelmingly, the very military that the United States trains and supplies—together with its paramilitary allies. Few know that the victims of the violence are, overwhelmingly, unarmed civilians, peasants, and workers, men, women, and children, whose crime is that their very presence stands in the way of the profits of the powerful.

Few people in the United States are aware of the global links in Colombia's violence, yet these global links are many. Colombia's coffee, oil, gold, bananas, flowers, emeralds, and coal, as well as Colombian cocaine, flow into world markets. Foreign companies such as Coca-Cola, Chiquita, Dole, Standard Oil, Occidental Petroleum, Exxon, Nestlé, Drummond, BHP Billiton, Glencore, Anglo American, and GreyStar control important sectors of Colombia's economy and reap important profits from their Colombian operations. International lending agencies such as the World Bank and the International Monetary Fund have pressed privatization on Colombia, meaning that the ability of the government to make decisions about the country's resources and economy continues to shrink.

How can these companies maintain their profits when peasants live on the land the companies want to mine, when workers organize for decent wages and benefits, when citizens demand a voice in the use of their country's resources? To answer this question is to uncover the sources of violence that are hidden to much of the U.S. public. Money flows from U.S. taxpayers to the U.S. government, to the Colombian military, to the paramilitaries; the latter two use these funds explicitly to remove any obstacles to the profits of foreign companies. Paramilitary incursions clear peasants from valuable land, such as the gold-rich areas of the Sur de Bolívar or Norte de Santander, opening it to foreign investors. Paramilitary forces patrol companies' premises, enter factories, and selectively kill workers who organize unions, as they have been accused of doing in the La Loma coal mine (owned by the Alabama-based Drummond Company), or Coca-Cola bottling plants, or Urabá's banana plantations. Colombian army units are specially trained to guard U.S.-owned facilities like Occidental Petroleum's Caño Limón-Coveñas oil pipeline.[1]

For the past twenty years, Colombian sociologist and journalist Alfredo Molano has worked to reveal the social and cultural effects of the violence in Colombia. As a teacher and scholar, as a journalist and author, and as a tireless advocate for human rights, Molano's name stands out in Colombian and international circles. Until now, however, the English speaking public has had little access to his work. Alfredo Molano's *The Dispossessed* brings us the voices of Colombians displaced by violence. These are intensely personal stories, yet they are also more than just individual stories. This volume contributes to the genre of *testimonio,* or testimony, a distinctively Latin American literary movement that flourished in the 1980s. The roots of Latin American testimonio date all the way back to the sixteenth-century Dominican friar Bartolomé de las Casas who, outraged by the violence unleashed by Spanish conquerors on the indigenous population of the so-called Indies, devoted his life to unearthing and recording the voices that the conquerors tried to silence. Testimonio is generally a personal story recorded by an outsider for a political purpose, to bring the voice of the voiceless to a larger public, to awaken the consciousness of the world to the violence, to try to stop it. Many of the testimonios of the 1980s came out of Central America, and they played an important role in awakening public awareness of, and solidarity with, Central American social movements.[2]

The people whose stories Molano tells are not social activists. They do not provide political or structural explanations of their lives; they do not tell stories of coming to consciousness. Yet together their stories add up to a powerful analysis of today's Colombia, and should indeed inspire readers to challenge the U.S. policies that continue to kill, impoverish, and displace the people of Colombia.

1 Human Rights Watch, *Colombia's Killer Networks: The Military-Paramilitary Partnership and the United States* (New York: Human Rights Watch, 1996); Michael McClintock, *Instruments of Statecraft: U.S. Guerrilla Warfare, Counterinsurgency, and Counterterrorism, 1940–1990* (New York: Pantheon Books, 1992); David Bacon, "The Colombian Connection: U.S. Aid Fuels Dirty War Against Unions," *In These Times*, July 23, 2001; Aram Roston, "It's the Real Thing: Murder," *The Nation*, September 3, 2001.

2 Elisabeth Burgos-Debray, *I, Rigoberta Menchu* (New York: Verso Books, 1987); Domitila Barrios de Chungara, *Let Me Speak! Testimony of Domitila, a Woman of the Bolivian Mines* (New York: Monthly Review Press, 1979); Lynn Stephen, *Hear My Testimony: María Teresa Tula, Human Rights Activist of El Salvador* (Boston: South End Press, 1994); Elvia Alvarado, *Don't be Afraid, Gringo: A Honduran Woman Speaks from the Heart* (New York: Perennial, 1989); Thomas F. Reed and Karen Brandow, *The Sky Never Changes: Testimonies from the Guatemalan Labor Movement* (Ithaca, NY: ILR Press, 1996).

Introduction
By Lance Selfa

To be dispossessed is to be evicted, ousted, or uprooted. The word used in Colombia to describe a similar state of being is *desterrado*. The verb *desterrar,* from which it is derived, means "to cast someone from territory or land by a judicial order or governmental decision."[1] It describes the more than three million Colombians dispossessed since 1985 living in ramshackle refugee camps, rural refugees living in urban slums, and others who have been forced to flee the country for their lives. For these people, leaving their land or the towns of their birth means more than "displacement" to some other part of the country. It often means losing their livelihoods, their family ties, and any sense of stability in their lives. And, while very few have actually received legally enforceable orders of expulsion, most know that the hand of the government and landowners—usually operating through shadowy networks of paramilitaries—lies behind the forces that put them to flight.

Haymarket Books welcomes the opportunity to bring *The Dispossessed,* published under the title *Desterrados* in Colombia in 2001, to an English-speaking audience for the first time. We are also honored that Alfredo Molano, one of the most respected journalists and scholars in Latin America, allowed us to publish Daniel Bland's fine translation of this work. We hope that it will increase Molano's audience in North America and that it will serve to educate the public about a country that did not receive its first comprehensive historical treatment in English until 1993.[2]

Molano's *Desterrados* is part of a cultural phenomenon of literature focused on themes of violence and displacement in Colombian life. This literature includes Laura Restrepo's *La multitud errante* (The Wandering Multitude), Marisol Gómez Giraldo's 2001 work also titled *Desterrados*, and Fernando Vallejo's *La virgen de los sicarios* (Our Lady of the Assassins), a 1994 novel that director Barbet Schroeder adapted into an award-winning 2000 film. María Helena Rueda explained the popularity of the literature of displacement in Colombia in the early 2000s:

> Displacement is a palpable and tragic reality. But it is also a metaphor for life today in Colombia. Colombia is a country that, for the people who live there, has been transformed into a foreign land. It is unrecognizable, not only because of violence, but because of other processes that have been strengthened in recent years. The state has weakened; there is an absence of ideological discourse to link people to a struggle for democracy; unemployment looms like a ghost; socioeconomic imbalances resulting from drug trafficking and corruption are profoundly unsettling; the bankruptcy of industries that could not survive free market reforms which liberated imports and the crashing of coffee prices—all of these phantoms are the life companions with whom the Colombian people have had to learn to co-exist in recent years.[3]

By early 2002, Molano's *Desterrados* had reached seventh in book sales in Colombia. Reviewers praised its honesty and willingness to reveal truths that polite society would rather have ignored. "These chronicles shake you to the core," wrote Luis

Barros Pavajeau in the online cultural review *La Esquina Regional.* "However, they are part of the other country, one that feels far from the large cities. A country that covers itself with a cloak of silence, to dodge the shame of a reality that still fills every corner."[4] Antonio Caballero, a columnist for the weekly *Semana*, cited the story of Toñito, related in "The Turkish Boat," in a broadside against the government's failure to protect the country's children from violence.[5]

When *Desterrados* appeared in Colombia, its author was marking his second year in exile from the country. As he describes in his personal memoir, "From Exile," Molano fled Colombia for Spain on Chistmas Day, 1998. He had become a target of the country's paramilitaries after serving as an adviser to the president's appointed commission charged with investigating the possibility of entering into peace negotiations with the guerrilla oppositions, the Revolutionary Armed Forces of Colombia (FARC) and the National Liberation Army (ELN). Through this work, Molano became increasingly outspoken about the obvious (but unacknowledged) collaboration between the Colombian armed forces and the right-wing paramilitaries, who carried out horrific massacres of peasants in the name of fighting the guerrillas. Spokesmen for the "paras" (as the paramilitaries are known) openly threatened Molano with death. Molano discovered that two suspicious men loitering outside his house were soldiers dressed in civilian clothes, and an armed forces commander assigned to protect him admitted that the army couldn't protect him from would-be assassins. The last straw came when paramilitaries, citing "irrefutable proof" that Molano was a "paraguerrilla," delivered a threat to the editorial offices of *El Espectador,* the liberal Bogotá newspaper where Molano writes his weekly column. After nearly five years in exile in Spain and the United States, Molano returned to Colombia in early 2004. Molano makes no secret of his identification with the political Left, but the charge that he is a "paraguerrilla" is absurd. As he told an American interviewer in 2000, he faced death threats because

> I am a man of the Left and of the university, more or less. I continue being very critical in Colombian society of the political system, including of the army and naturally the paramilitaries. This doesn't mean I'm totally in agreement with the guerrilla, although I agree with them on many things. I agree with agrarian reform. I agree with the reforms they've proposed for the army. I agree with the reforms of the media and the justice system. But naturally I don't agree with everything. First, because the guerrilla has Stalinist roots. They are military forces and this gives a lot of force to authoritarian tendencies. I place myself at a distance from that. But my critiques of the system, of the great landowners, of the ranchers, of the army, of the paramilitaries, these are what caused the threats. And the threats grew until I saw that not only was I in danger but my family and those close to me.[6]

Molano is one of Colombia's leading public intellectuals, the winner of major awards for his scholarly and journalistic work. A trained sociologist with an advanced degree from the École Pratiques des Hautes Études in Paris, he served in executive positions in several nongovernmental organizations addressing issues of environmental and rural development before taking a position with the government's peace commission. Although well recognized for his academic publications, Molano turned to a new arena—newspaper and television journalism—in the late 1980s. Since 1991, he has written a weekly column in *El Espectador*. In 1993, he won the Simón Bolívar Journalism Prize for an episode of the television documentary "Travesías" about

Colombia's indigenous in the town of Chenche. Journalism gave him a wider audience than those who had read his technical reports. It carried a cost, as well:

> I think people began reading me with a mixture of surprise and disbelief. Gradually, though, they began to feel something and like—or dislike—the people I described in my chronicles and stories and in my weekly column. But that created a problem because as more readers became interested and began to defend my notions of the country, more enemies appeared. (p. 43)

Molano found increased interest in his work because many of his readers could empathize with the human stories he told. As Aviva Chomsky's foreword points out, Molano's trademark style is firmly rooted in the Latin American tradition of testimonial literature. This method imbues Molano's work with an authenticity and a radicalism—not in the sense of a political tract, but that of "going to the root of the problem." Molano's work holds a mirror up to Colombian society, trying to present it as it *is*. He captures the point of view of ordinary people—from peasant activists to drug couriers. His method brings to mind Russian revolutionary V.I. Lenin's admonition that "one must always try to be as radical as reality itself."[7]

The view of Colombia that emerges from Molano's *crónica* is that of a country where deadly violence accompanies everyday life like the rain or sun. In "Ángela," the young narrator dwells mostly on memories of her childhood. Violence only intervenes, initially, as a disruption of her play: "We used to go down to the river a lot to cool off, especially in the afternoon, until my father forbid it because of the bodies that began to float by. He didn't want us to see them" (p. 69). In "The Garden," another narrator remembers, thirty-seven years after the event and rather matter-

of-factly, the day assassins broke into her first communion celebration. Their victim's blood splattered across her white dress.
The violence erupts and engulfs the individuals, who often
admit they have no idea how they could have become ensnared.
Ángela's father realizes he has to flee after paramilitaries accuse
him of ferrying guerrillas across a river. "But my father didn't
know who they were," says Ángela (p. 70). The four protagonists
of "Silences" seem more interested in living out their retirement
years in Boca del Cajambre than in the conflicts around them.
Yet paramilitaries murder old Ánibal after he makes the mistake
of sharing Christmas Eve dinner, drinks, and a shower with
members of a guerrilla unit.

For the most part, the people who tell Molano their stories
are apolitical, in the sense that most of them are not political
activists or guerrillas. But this should not blind us to the fact
that the violence and the displacement have very clear political
and economic roots.[8] Documenting these political, social, and
economic roots of the *desterrados* is the contribution of Mabel
González Bustelo's essay "Desterrados: Forced Displacement in
Colombia." González Bustelo, a Spanish journalist and researcher
with the Centro de la Investigación para la Paz (Peace Research
Center) in Madrid, helps us to grasp both the magnitude and
the causes of the problem of forced displacement in Colombia,
clearly linked to a neoliberal economic model that focuses on
Colombia's export industries:

> Forced displacement is a phenomenon linked to the history
> of Colombia and to the country's unfinished historical
> processes. The economic and political elite have used dis-
> placement to "homogenize" the population in a given area
> and to maintain and expand large estates. Currently, the
> pressure exerted by the neoliberal model to increase capital

circuits has made the process more difficult by introducing factors that change the value of the land. As such, people are not displaced "by violence"; rather, violence is the tool used to expel the population. The true causes for displacement are hidden behind the violence. The reasons for displacement include strategic control of military and political areas, restructuring of local and regional powers, control or disruption of social movements, control of production and extraction activities (of natural resources and minerals), mega-projects, expansion of stockbreeding estates and agricultural industry, control of illicit crops, etc.[9]

The current war between the Colombian state, the paramilitaries, and the guerrillas must be viewed in this context. González Bustelo has written that Von Clausewitz's famous aphorism can be adapted to Colombia today as "war is the continuation of economics through other means." This phrase not only describes the historic employment of private landlord armies to seize prime farmland, but also today's neoliberal policies that slash state education and health services to such a point that huge areas of the country seem untouched by any state presence except the military. In this "Wild West" atmosphere, paramilitaries and guerrillas can fill the void so that entire regions of the country become immune to Bogotá's influence. Neoliberal policies forcing competition between small Colombian farmers and international agribusiness drove more than five million farmers off their lands in the 1990s. In many cases, farmers turned to the production of coca and other illicit crops as a means to survive. In other cases, landlords hired paramilitaries to drive farmers out and replaced production of food crops with livestock. This is why Molano once described Colombia as "a country where a cow is worth more than a person."[10]

Another aspect of globalization and neoliberalism is the role of international capital in the chain of events that forces thousands off their lands. Colombia is one of the richest natural-resource-producing countries in the world. Multinationals investing in minerals, cash crops, petroleum, and other products contribute to the pressure to expel populations that get in the way of their unfettered access to the country's resources. As González Bustelo shows, British Petroleum financed paramilitaries. In the late 1990s, Occidental Petroleum lobbied Congress to expand the area covered under Plan Colombia to places where the company had its investments. One study estimated that 84 percent of the displaced come from areas that produce 78 percent of the country's oil revenues.[11]

If violence is part of doing business in Colombia, both international and Colombian firms feel no qualms about employing it to repress activities, such as labor and peasant organizing, that might impede their search for profits. Human Rights Watch and the AFL-CIO confirm that Colombia is the most dangerous place in the world for trade unionists to organize. Since 1991, more than three thousand trade unionists died at the hands of assassins.[12] Likewise, "Forced migrations take place in areas where people are not politically active (as shown in their electoral participation) but very socially active (protests, demonstrations), proving the high social costs of the displacements," González Bustelo shows.[13] Especially targeted are areas with traditions of farmworker, peasant, and indigenous rights organizing.

The testimonies presented in *The Dispossessed* describe in the most personal terms how these larger economic and social processes play out in ordinary people's lives. Paramilitaries enter the scene of "The Defeat" as a protection force for "Don

Enrique Ortiz, a businessman who bought all the wood he could get his hands on to sell to Cartones Colombianos" (p.56), a major cardboard manufacturing multinational. Harvesting the wood in question was illegal, and "finding (out) about that little business ... proved to be the beginning of the end for Diego and his friend Aníbal," the protagonists of the story (p. 56). The drug economy—and the paramilitaries' fight to control it— figures prominently in a number of the *crónicas*. The narrator in "Silences" recounts his participation in a strike on a banana plantation. The plantation bosses call in the local military commander who warns the banana workers that they might be taken for guerrilla sympathizers. The following day, the narrator finds the bodies of two union leaders hanging from a banana tree. The strike was crushed, and the narrator flees the plantation, remarking, "No one was ever punished for those murders, and the bosses never lost as much as a minute's sleep over them" (p. 87). Yet, for this narrator, paramilitary violence didn't intimidate him forever. "Silences" stands out as an account of someone who not only learns to cope with the violence, but to stand up to it. He becomes a campesino organizer who finishes his narrative on a note of hope and defiance: "As for me, I'm still with my people. We've stopped running and decided to resist. Without weapons or a thirst for vengeance but with the land we've worked and made something of together. The land that is us all" (p. 96).

The stories also document guerrilla relations with the rural population. They paint a picture that neither echoes the Colombian (and U.S.) government's fulminations against "narco-terrorists," nor excuses the guerrillas for their sometimes brutal treatment of their presumed constituents. It is notable that the narrator of "Silences," who clearly identifies himself as a church-based activist, describes this dynamic in the field of peasant organizing: "When the church in its way, and the guerrillas in their way, threw in with the people, the paramilitaries and the army appeared" (p. 95). In other words, the narrator saw himself and the guerrillas to be fighting on the same side, the side of the campesinos. To the narrator of "Nubia, La Catira," the guerrillas were defenders of campesinos, meting out frontier justice against bandits who preyed on coffee farmers. Nubia says, "The guerrillas were good people, not rude or bad-mannered…. The guerrillas taught me to read and write and I always wanted them to take me to their camp" (p. 179). On the other hand, we also see the guerrillas as inflexible and domineering. Ninfa, the narrator of "The Garden," loses both her father and husband to guerrilla executions. In both cases, the guerrillas are deceived into thinking the condemned to be collaborators with the paras, but this is no consolation to Ninfa: "I'll never forgive the guerrillas for not trying to find out more about what happened, about our mistake. We acted in good faith. The *paracos* tricked us, and, what's more, they tricked the guerrillas as well into committing a crime" (p. 135).

Despite this, Molano's informants leave no doubt that they believe the paramilitaries and their collaborators in the police and military to be the chief source of violence in the countryside. Statistics back up Molano's informants. Right-wing paramilitaries account for two to three times the number of forced displacements than the guerrillas have caused, according to the United Nations. One 2001 report estimated that paramilitaries account for 79 percent of all human rights violations against civilian populations, compared to 16 percent of human rights violations attributed to guerrillas.[14] These paramilitary actions contributed to conditions that caused the majority of 412,000 to flee their homes in 2002, and an additional 175,000 to flee in 2003, according to the nongovernmental Consultancy on Human Rights and Displacement (CODHES). Given the prevalence of forced displacement in the countryside, it is understandable why each story revolves around a horrific act of paramilitary violence. "Whenever there were bodies in the river," the child Ángela says matter-of-factly, "the paramilitaries showed up" (p. 73).

The clear collaboration between the official military, the police, and the paramilitaries is well-documented. In fact, some observers have likened the increase in paramilitary activity to a "privatization" of the state's repressive apparatus, providing the government with "plausible deniability" while it seeks to wipe out guerrilla and other challenges to its rule.[15] A January 2004 Human Rights Watch report states the case unequivocally:

> Although the Colombian government describes these ties as the acts of individuals and not a matter of policy or even tolerance, the range of abuses clearly depends on the approval, collusion, and tolerance of high-ranking officers. The Uribe Administration has yet to arrest paramilitary leaders or high-ranking members of the Armed Forces credibly alleged to collaborate with abusive paramilitary groups. Arrest statistics provided by the military are overwhelmingly skewed toward low-ranking members of paramilitary groups or individuals whose participation in these groups is alleged, not proven.[16]

By some estimates, the paramilitaries control as much as one half of the country's illicit drug trade, producing revenue of $1–$2 billion annually. Therefore, the paras are not a ragtag band, but a virtual, and well-financed, state within a state.

Human rights activists charge that the Uribe government's plans to accept surrenders of paramilitary leaders and the disbanding of their units are either a smokescreen for international consumption or a step toward the legalization of the paramilitaries and their open integration into the armed forces.[17] The question posed by narrator Osiris, who loses a husband and son to the paras, remains unanswered: "Where do you demand justice when the authorities who pick up the bodies are the same ones who kill them? Who do you denounce the crime to if the authorities are all smeared with blood?" (p. 159).

When people are forced to flee, they end up in camps for displaced persons, other towns, or as country people living in the slums of major cities like Bogotá or Medellín. *The Dispossessed* captures their disorientation of living as strangers where they are often not welcome. Perhaps the most dramatic of these accounts is the story of the boy Toñito, told in "The Turkish Boat." Fleeing a paramilitary massacre of his village in the Chocó region—a massacre that leaves him an orphan—he takes a riverboat all the way to the Caribbean port city of Cartagena. There, residing in the Mandela slum with thousands of other *desterrados,* he describes his life: "I lived with a gang in the street. We hustled anywhere we could" (p. 110). He and his gang run afoul of the local police and mafia, compelling him to stow away on a Turkish vessel bound for New York. Toñito barely survives that escape attempt, as the ship's captain orders the stowaway thrown overboard.

The *desterrados'* move from the countryside to the city introduces them to a different set of challenges than those they faced in their villages. There are the politicians and priests who demand payoffs for their help in finding housing, food, and job assistance for the displaced. There is the danger of street crime—from petty theft to murderous drug turf battles. Consumer goods are more available in the city, but food is less plentiful and more expensive. And the displaced face racism and discrimination. Osiris, of Afro-Colombian descent, recounts an incident in which a man, firing shots at her family's home in the middle of the night, taunts them: "Come out of there, you displaced sons-of-bitches, fucking guerrillas! Come out and die!" Osiris puts on a brave face: "It turned out to be one of the neighbors who'd had too much to drink and decided to make fun of us for being displaced. It was a joke. But jokes have their poison and drunks say what they really feel. Things here are difficult" (p. 170).

The question of violence and displacement

"The roots of Colombia's crisis lie in its historically weak state, a divided ruling class, and a closed two-party political system that has blocked any participation or voice from the mass of the population,"[18] write Tristin Adie and Paul D'Amato, summarizing the main reasons for the violent nature of Colombian society. For the first century and a half of Colombia's existence as an independent state, the elite-based Liberal and Conservative Parties, whose influence reached from Bogotá to every rural town, rotated in and out of government with a regularity lampooned in Gabriel Garcia Márquez's *One Hundred Years of Solitude*. Periodic party competition led to armed conflict, with militias of Liberals and Conservatives squaring off in rural areas. Throughout most of this time, the mass of the population remained excluded from the political spoils, or, in the case of some peasants, remained tied to the Liberals or Conservatives.

This began to change in the 1930s, when, during the Great Depression, labor and peasant organizing put pressure on the political system. The Liberal governments of the 1930s enacted measures providing for social security and workers' rights akin to U.S. president Franklin Roosevelt's New Deal or the state-led reforms of Mexican president Lázaro Cárdenas. As in the United States, this period of reform was short-lived. The Second World War and the subsequent Cold War put a damper on popular aspirations, giving the Colombian Right an opening to roll back the 1930s reforms. President Alfonso López Pumarejo, who had played the FDR role in the 1930s, returned to power in the war years only to lead a retrenchment in the reforms he had championed. This ignited a populist movement inside (and outside) the Liberal Party, in which the Left, workers, and peasant organizations rallied behind the charismatic politician Jorge Eliécer Gaitán. Gaitán came in third in the presidential elections of 1946, not far behind the official Liberal candidate. He looked to be in a strong position to win the 1950 election. However, on April 9, 1948, an assassin cut down Gaitán on a Bogotá street. The assassination ignited the *Bogotazo,* weeks of mass rioting in the capital and beyond, as Gaitán supporters accused the Conservatives or official Liberals of murdering their leader. After a brief respite, the violence reignited, this time engulfing the country in a cycle, which has since been called *La Violencia,* lasting through 1958. Eduardo Galeano describes La Violencia:

> The violence began with a confrontation between Liberal and Conservative Parties, but the dynamic of class hostilities steadily sharpened its class struggle character.... When [Gaitán] was shot dead, the hurricane was unleashed. First the spontaneous Bogotazo—an uncontrollable human tide in the streets of the capital; then the violence spread to the countryside, where bands organized by the Conservatives had for some time been sowing terror. The bitter taste of hatred, long in the peasants' mouths, provoked an explosion; the government sent police and soldiers to cut off testicles, slash pregnant women's bellies, and throw babies into the air to catch on bayonet points.... Liberal Party sages shut them-

selves in their homes, never abandoning their good manners and the gentlemanly tone of their manifestoes.... It was a war of incredible cruelty and it became worse as it went on, feeding the lust for vengeance.[19]

La Violencia took the lives of as many as 300,000 Colombians. It came to an end only when the Liberals and Conservatives agreed to a National Front pact in 1958. In the pact, the two parties agreed to trade the presidency every four years and to divide up the spoils of government between them. This arrangement held until 1974. As Jenny Pearce has explained,

> The state was ... literally carved up by the traditional parties. In addition to alternating the presidency between them for 16 years, all legislative bodies and public corporations ... cabinet offices, judicial posts and posts at all levels of public administration were to be distributed by agreement between the two parties.
>
> No expression of social conflict was permitted outside the control of the two traditional parties.[20]

While the National Front governments quelled the interparty conflicts, they did not end the peasant insurgencies sparked during La Violencia. In the 1950s, Conservative governments—with backing from the United States—launched major military operations against peasants who wanted to protect and extend the land reforms of the 1930s. These military operations stimulated the organization of peasant self-defense forces into guerrilla armies in which Colombia's small Communist Party played a role. Focused on the nearly uninhabited departments (a subnational unit of government similar to a state government in the United States) of Meta and Caquetá, these peasant armies set up "independent republics" intended to allow peasants to work the land free of interference from the central government. But the central government and great landlords had no intention of ceding their authority to the independent republics. Instead they defined the peasant leaders as "communists and bandits" and set about reconquering the land from them. As Molano wrote in an important 1992 study of this process, "The only possible outcome was war. One by one the republics fell to the army, and once they were under government control the land became concentrated in the hands of the large landowners."[21]

Government and landlord assaults provoked a counter-mobilization among the peasants and others who found themselves locked out of the country's closed political system. "Seeing that it would be impossible to break through the rigid political and agrarian structures using legal means, the opposition declared an armed rebellion. During the same period other guerrilla forces, the National Liberation Army (ELN) in 1964 and the People's Liberation Army (EPL) in 1967, were created, and the big land-owners dominated the country's economy."[22] In 1966, several guerrilla forces tied to the Communist Party fused into the FARC. Through many political, ideological, and military twists and turns, the FARC and the ELN have established themselves today as the most durable guerrilla forces in Colombia. However, they have not been the only guerrilla challengers to the Colombian government. In the 1970s and 1980s, the urban-based guerrillas, the M-19, rose in prominence. But the M-19's seizure of the Palace of Justice in 1985—which resulted in the immolation of the Supreme Court and the deaths of many judges, lawyers, and ordinary citizens—provoked a backlash against it. Even though the Colombian military leveled the Palace of Justice in its assault on M-19 guerrillas, the government seized the initiative to deliver a crushing blow to the M-19. A 1989 government amnesty to

M-19 members brought former guerrillas into the electoral arena and propelled one M-19 leader, Antonio Navarro Wolf, into a position with the Colombian government in the 1990s. However, Wolf's transition from guerrilla to mainstream politician was the exception. The majority of M-19 members, as well as thousands of guerrillas from the FARC and other formations, took seriously the government's 1984 invitation to lay down their arms and to compete in the electoral arena. They formed Unión Patriótica (UP), a left-of-center electoral front, in 1985 to compete in the 1986 presidential and newly approved local government elections.[23] Looking forward to the 1986 elections, FARC leader Manuel Marulanda, known by his *nom de guerre* Tirofijo ("Sureshot"), spoke of his desire to return to political life as a local town counselor. But the government and the armed Right reneged on their promises. The false dawn of the 1986 elections "proved to be a great deception; the UP was literally annihilated as many of its leaders and hundreds of its candidates for office were murdered."[24] In fact, human rights workers have documented more than 3,000 murders of UP activists. With the UP experiment a shambles, the guerrillas returned to the hills and took up arms again.

It goes without saying that this history forms the backdrop to the stories of the *desterrados* told here. In some cases, the historical connections are more direct. The narrator of "The Garden" relates that her father was a guerrilla during *La Violencia*. "They turned over their weapons to the army during the [1953–57] Rojas government—getting nothing in return that time—and that's when he met my mother" (p. 119). The narrator of "Silences," describes his father as a guerrilla who joined a Liberal unit founded "to avenge the murder of ... Jorge Eliécer Gaitán" (p. 82).

The mother of Nubia, La Catira, was president of the Unión Patriótica party in her town, chosen, no doubt, in recognition of her work in pressuring the government to deliver roads, health care, and schools. Sadly, her mother was one of the thousands of UP activists who died at the hands of military-controlled death squads that wanted to close Colombia's "opening to democracy."

As the guerrilla war began again, two new elements jumped into the vortex of violence: the drug cartels and the paramilitaries. In fact, the two rose side by side, as the major drug cartels in Medillín and Cali financed and armed many of the original paramilitary forces. Colombian peasant farmers, facing ruin and poverty in the 1970s and 1980s, turned to coca production as a lucrative and easily transportable crop. Guerrillas levied "war taxes" on middlemen who facilitated transport of the coca from the fields to the cartels, allowing them to finance a range of social services for the rural poor. But the cartel leaders invested part of their superprofits in land and cattle—placing them in league with the traditional enemies of the rural poor and guerrillas. And when guerrillas turned to kidnapping and ransoming of wealthy "narco-landowners," the druglords created "death to kidnappers" paramilitary groups to fight the guerrillas. The drug cartels' creation of death squads overlapped with the traditional oligarchy's opposition to any negotiated settlement with the guerrillas. Forces inside the military opposed to the guerrillas also took advantage of a loophole in Colombian law allowing them to create "self-defense forces," or *autodefensas*, private militias armed by the military. The result of all this was a huge increase from the 1980s to today in paramilitary activity, including massacres, disappearances, and forced displacements.[25]

Since the drug cartels, the traditional oligarchy, and the military represented an alliance of sectors of Colombia's ruling class, it wasn't long before paramilitary activity became directed not just at guerrillas, but at any force inside Colombian society that dared to challenge the status quo. Human rights workers, trade unionists, peasant leaders, left-of-center politicians, and others having little or nothing to do with guerrilla activity became targets of the paramilitaries. In the cities—especially in the slum areas where many of the displaced concentrate when they flee to urban areas— "social cleansing" by hired assassins *(sicarios)* annually murders hundreds of street children, prostitutes, and others deemed "undesirable."[26] An account of just such an incident of "social cleansing" forms the core of the story in "The Turkish Boat."

Given the horrific conditions and the climate of repression that so many Colombians experience, the continued resilience of labor and peasant movements and the desire of ordinary Colombians to forge a better future is remarkable. Despite the conditions of civil war and the government's penchant to label all opposition as "terrorism," more than two million Colombians engaged in strikes to protest austerity measures in 1999. In 2003, Colombian voters defeated a referendum with which President Alvaro Uribe attempted to ram through huge spending cuts and to win approval for near-dictatorial powers. At the same time, voters chose members of the Independent Left Pole, a coalition of trade union, human rights, and social movement activists, to run many of the country's major cities and departments, including Bogotá.

The United States and the violence in Colombia today

What happens in the Colombian *cordillera* may seem distant from the everyday lives of North Americans. But connections between Colombia and North America—and the United States in particular—are not hard to establish. The United States has actively intervened in Colombian affairs throughout the country's modern history. As a leading producer of raw materials, including oil, and with its geographic position at the crossroads of Central America and Latin America, Colombia has long figured in U.S. strategic planning. In the early 1900s, the United States helped to sponsor a secession movement in Colombia's northwest that resulted in the creation of the country of Panama— just in time for the new nation to cooperate with U.S. plans to build a canal there. In the period of the Cold War, Colombia became a major recipient of U.S. foreign aid and the major testing ground for the Alliance for Progress.[27] Economic and development assistance combined aid to Colombia's armed forces. The administration of President John F. Kennedy advised the Colombian military to "select civilian and military personnel ... as necessary [to] execute paramilitary, sabotage and/or terrorist activities against known Communist proponents. It should be backed by the United States."[28] To fulfill that goal, the United States trained as many as ten thousand officers in the Colombian armed forces and security services at the infamous School of the Americas (recently renamed the Western Hemisphere Institute for Security Cooperation).

In the 1990s, Colombia once again took center stage in U.S. policy toward Latin America, as the country became the cockpit for the U.S. "war on drugs." As the Cold War ended, U.S. policymakers cast around for new rationales for U.S. military intervention that had been justified as necessary to confront "communism." In Latin America, "fighting drugs," "narcoterrorists," and "narcoguerrillas" filled the bill. As a former Reagan administration defense official explained, "Getting help from the military on drugs used to be like pulling teeth. Now everybody's looking around to say, 'Hey, how can we justify these forces?' And the answer they're coming up with is drugs."[29] Yet, as many observers of U.S.-Colombian policy have pointed out, the focus of the anti-drug war has overlapped closely with guerrilla-controlled areas—even though U.S. and Colombian officials agreed that the guerrillas were not the country's main cocaine traffickers. In other words, the war on drugs is essentially a counterinsurgency program intended to defeat the guerrillas. In 2002, the Bush administration made this rationale official when it announced that its Colombia policy would be conducted under the rubric of fighting "terrorism."

Today, Colombia is the third-largest recipient of U.S. military aid, behind Israel and Egypt. Between 2000 and 2003, the United States spent $2.4 billion in aid for Colombia, 80 percent of it directed to the military and police. In 2002, the U.S. authorized $99 million to pay for protection of the Caño Limón-Coveñas oil pipeline, with almost half of its capacity dedicated to U.S.-based Occidental Petroleum.[30] In January 2004, the Bush administration released $34 million to the Colombian armed forces, certifying that Colombia had fulfilled State Department human rights requirements to break with paramilitary organizations. The government of Alvaro Uribe, elected in 2002 on a platform promising harsh repression of the guerrilla opposition, remains one of the chief allies of the Bush administration in Latin America. In these ways, the U.S. government stands out as the chief external backer of the armed forces—and, by extension, their paramilitary allies—in Colombia. These are precisely the forces overwhelmingly responsible for turning millions of their countrymen and women into *desterrados.*

Luis Adolfo Cardona is one such person whom I have met in Chicago. Luis Adolfo was an organizer in the National Food Workers' Union, SINALTRAINAL, and a forklift operator at the Coca-Cola plant in Antioquia before he had to flee his country. His story is similar to those recorded in *The Dispossessed.* Narrowly escaping a kidnapping by paramilitaries in 1996, he fled to Bogotá. After receiving death threats there, he fled the country. The AFL-CIO Solidarity Center's program to protect Colombian trade unionists offered him and his family refuge in the United States. In late 2003, he won political asylum in the United States. He works tirelessly, speaking to union members, students, and church groups about the repression of trade union-ists and of the paramilitaries' connections to Coca-Cola and other U.S. companies. While human rights reports can describe the repression in Colombia, no one can better convey what it really means than someone like Luis Adolfo or the people whom Alfredo Molano has recorded in this book. We publish *The Dispossessed* in North America in the belief that if Americans knew the full extent of the misery that their government sup-ports in Colombia, they wouldn't stand for it.

"Maybe it would be better for us if we didn't talk about what happened, about our history," says Osiris, the narrator of the chronicle named for her. "But if we don't tell people about it, all of our dead will remain dead forever. We may have to bury them but that doesn't mean we are ever going to forget them" (p. 174). In *The Dispossessed*, people like Osiris help us not only to remember the dead, but motivate us to do what we can to change the conditions that led to their killings.

1 According to the first definition offered in the *Diccionario de la Lengua Española,* 21st edition (Madrid: Real Academia Española, 2001).

2 David Bushnell, *The Making of Modern Colombia: A Nation in Spite of Itself* (Berkeley: University of California, 1993).

3 María Helena Rueda, "Chronicles of the Banished: Displacement and Popular Identity in Colombia," *GSC Quarterly,* no. 4, Spring 2002, Social Science Resource Council, Washington, D.C.

4 For the sales ranking of the book, see http://www.losandes.com.ar/2002/0403/ suplementos/cultura/nota68154_1.htm. Quotation is from a review of Desterrados by Luis Barros Pavajeau, La Esquina Regional, diciembre 2002–febrero 2003, at http://www.laesquinaregional.com.

5 Antonio Caballero, "Niños infelices," *Semana,* July 19, 2001, at http:// www.semana.com/archivo/articulosView.jsp?id=18946.

6 "Hidden Motives for a War," *NARCO News Bulletin,* August 7, 2000, at http:// www.narconews.com/exiled.html.

7 See Alexander Cockburn, "Radical as Reality," *Green Left Weekly* (Australia) at http://www.greenleft.org.au/back/1991/37/37p13.htm. The quotation is attributed to the 1927 memoir of Valeriu Marcu, *Lenin: 30 Years of Russia* (Berlin: Paul List/ Verlag, 1927).

8 "The term 'displaced' denounces the intention to mask one of the most tragic and bloodthirsty episodes of our time. The truth is that people do not move: they are moved, exiled, expelled, forced to flee and hide. Another method used to conceal this fact consists in seeing it as if it were the result of clashes between two new actors: the guerrillas and the paramilitary. Nevertheless, population expulsions are but an old resource used by the system, which, by pointing to illegal armed groups as the original source of the problem, exonerates the Regime and above all the Armed Forces from all responsibility." See Alfredo Molano, "Desterrados," en *Papeles de cuestiones internacionales,* no. 70, Spring 2000, Centro de Investigación para la Paz, Madrid.

9 Mabel González Bustelo, "Desterrados: Forced Displacement in Colombia," in this volume, p. 232.

10 Cited in Nectalí Ariza Ariza, "El Conflicto Colombiano y la Coyuntura Internacional, at http://www.ccoo.illes.balears.net/asociaciones/pau/observatori/ colombiaanalisis.pdf.

11 González Bustelo, p. 209.

12 See "International Union Body Makes Breakthrough with Colombian Authorities," February 3, 2004, International Confederation of Free Trade Unions, at http:// www.icftu.org.

13 González Bustelo, p. 210.

14 See a summary of the relevant data in Norwegian Refugee Council, "Profile of Internal Displacement: Colombia," February 2004, 35ff.

15 Ricardo Vargas Meza, "The FARC, the War and the Crisis of the State," *NACLA Report on the Americas* 31(5), March–April 1998, p. 23, and "The Wars Within: Counterinsurgency in Chiapas and Colombia," *op. cit.*, p. 6.

16 Quoted from "Colombia: Briefing to the 60th Session of the UN Commission on Human Rights, at http://hrw.org/english/docs/2004/01/29/colomb7124_txt.htm.

17 Juan Forero, "800 in Colombia Lay Down Arms, Kindling Peace Hopes," *New York Times*, November 26, 2003.

18 Tristin Adie and Paul D'Amato, "Colombia: The Terrorist State," *International Socialist Review*, no. 10 (Winter 2000), p. 21.

19 Eduardo Galeano, *Open Veins of Latin America: Five Centuries of the Pillage of a Continent* (New York: Monthly Review Press, 1973), pp. 116–17.

20 Jenny Pearce, quoted in Adie and D'Amato, p. 22.

21 Alfredo Molano, "Violence and Land Colonization," *Violence in Colombia: The Contemporary Crisis in Historical Perspective*, Charles Bergquist, Ricardo Penaranda, and Gonzalo Sanchez, eds. (Wilmington: Scholarly Resources, 1992), p. 199.

22 Alfredo Molano, "The Evolution of the FARC: A Guerrilla Group's Long History," *NACLA Report on the Americas* 34(2), September–October 2000. While the FARC and ELN remain active today, the majority of EPL members surrendered their arms in the early 1990s to participate in "above-ground" political activity.

23 Before 1986, the central government in Bogotá appointed local government officials. The national congress allowed local government elections in 1986 and the change was ratified permanently in the 1991 federal constitution.

24 Frank Safford and Marco Palacios, *Colombia: Fragmented Land, Divided Society* (New York: Oxford University Press, 2002), p. 356.

25 See Garry Leech, "Fifty Years of Violence," *Colombia Journal Online*, at http://www.colombiajournal.org/fiftyyearsofviolence.htm.

26 Ibid.

27 The Alliance for Progress was one of the Kennedy administration's responses to the 1959 Cuban Revolution: A program of loans to encourage economic development and private enterprise in Latin America. For more on the program, see John Gerassi, *The Great Fear in Latin America* (New York: Collier Books, 1965).

28 Quote in Noam Chomsky, *The New Military Humanism* (Monroe, Maine: Common Courage Press, 1999), p. 50.

29 Lawrence Korb, quoted in Peter Dale Scott and Jonathan Marshall, *Cocaine Politics: Drugs, Armies, and the CIA in Central America* (Berkeley: University of California Press, 1998), p. 3.

30 All figures from "Los Estados Unidos y Colombia, 2003: Una mirada a las cifras," Consultoria para los derechos humanos y desplazamiento (CODHES), available online at http://www.codhes.org.co.

THE DISPOSSESSED
Chronicles of the Desterrados of Colombia

Chapter 1

From Exile

I decided to write this book about three years ago when I opened the door to my apartment in Barcelona on a sad and dark afternoon in February. The silence struck me in the face and the emptiness, I confess, made my convictions waver. The statements I'd made to my readers, my children, and my friends, in order to respond to the death threats I received from the paramilitaries, were all behind me. They were neither the only nor the most dangerous threats. Paramilitarism is a time-worn strategy of a powerful sector of the Colombian establishment that has been used to frustrate attempts to achieve a civil solution to the country's armed conflict. Almost every campesino in Colombia can say that his father or his uncle or his grandfather was killed by the army or police, by the paramilitaries, or by the guerrillas. It is the diabolical inertia of the violence that, since before the assassination of Gaitán in 1948, has claimed more than a million lives.

My exile really began, however, when I put aside my books, stopped writing technical reports, and gave up the pretense of being able to understand our reality from behind a desk. The break came in the early 1980s, when I met an old woman who told me about her life and how she had spent all of it fleeing. Her grandparents had been taken away by Liberal troops during the "long wars of the nineteen hundreds and no one ever knew who won those battles because they never came back." Her story was so passionate that sociological treatises and Colombian history books lost much of their meaning for me after I heard it. I realized the way to understand wasn't to study people but to listen to them. And I decided, almost obsessively and using any pretext I could, to travel the length and breadth of the country in order to shatter the academic and official view of its history.

People told me thousands of stories and there was, and is, a common element to all of them: the forced displacement of people for political reasons and economic gain. The wealthy accused campesinos of being Liberals or Conservatives or communists in order to force them to flee and take their land. The spoils of war in Colombia have always been paid in land, and our history is the history of an incessant, almost uninter-rupted, displacement.

I wrote about what I saw and what people told me. I used a

tape recorder or a notebook and I even tried filming. Though written in the language of nineteenth-century travelers, the stories reached few people. Very few. A book printing in Colombia rarely exceeds three thousand copies and I was unsatisfied. The world the campesinos had shown me was being seen by the same circle of people. That was how by first putting in a finger, then a hand, and then finally, my whole arm, I arrived at newspapers.

I think people began reading me with a mixture of surprise and disbelief. Gradually, though, they began to feel something and like or dislike the people I described in my chronicles, stories, and weekly column. But that created a problem because as more readers became interested and began to defend my notions of the country, more enemies appeared. And my travels became more difficult. The stories, simple as they were, were denunciations of a landowner, a political strongman, a "competent" authority, an army captain, or a guerrilla commander, and the circle began to constrict as the weeks passed.

My travels also got more dangerous because the areas I visited—the frontier regions of colonization where coca and *amapola* are grown—were becoming more and more violent. The confrontation there between a formal and impeccably legal order and the "real" country, which believes only in itself, is played out every day in a multitude of violences. It wasn't only the *colonos* who had found a way of life by replacing traditional crops with illegal ones. The guerrillas had a treasure chest from extorting money from drug middlemen and traffickers, and the police and army enriched themselves by repressing the whole business. Everyone was taking a piece of the pie, and, in truth, no one had a right to throw the first stone. But some people began to do just that and blame those of us who saw the problem and denounced it and who understood how hypocritical it was to accuse only the guerrillas of drug trafficking when the reality was—and is—that they financed part of their activities with the money they extorted from the drug kingpins.

During this time, I was appointed external adviser to the peace counselor by the Samper government, a position that enabled me to continue voicing my opinions without them being associated with government policy. There was a possibility the guerrillas would begin talks with the government; the only precondition was the demilitarization of the town of La Uribe, a symbolic region for the FARC. After carrying out some political consultations, the government expressed its intention to go ahead with this but was faced with two obstacles: first, the crisis stemming from the existence of drug money in the 1994 electoral campaign, which placed President Samper on the defensive, and, second, the government's decision to license civilians so they could arm themselves and collaborate with the armed forces. In practice, this measure served to reinforce paramilitarism by helping set up armed groups, called *Convivir* (to live together), paid for by large landowners, many of whom were drug traffickers. These two circumstances began to weaken the government's position with the guerrillas and to make the demilitarization they asked for more difficult.

Meanwhile, I continued writing an opinion column in *El Espectador*, in which I denounced massacres the paramilitaries had committed, criticized the government for its weakness in the peace process, and, above all, pointed to the growing autonomy of the military from the civilian power in the country as the cause of the problems. I also commented on how nefarious the often-used doctrine of the "narco-guerrilla" had become for peace in Colombia. It was a term coined by a former American ambassador in Colombia that had been embraced wholeheartedly by the military, the right wing of both political parties, and, above all, by the media. My critical opinions earned me the open animosity of the country's right wing and the military, which began suggesting I was an "intellectual defender" of the guerrillas. In reality, I was simply stating publicly what I had seen and heard in those frontier zones where coca and amapola were being grown. I denounced not only the extortion the guerrillas were involved in but also the military's ties to the drug traffickers and links to the paramilitaries. It was a one-sided fight and one, I admit, I was only able to stay involved in thanks to the freedom the government gave me to say what I thought, even when I disagreed with its own positions. In similar fashion, my editors at *El Espectador* never removed so much as a comma from any of my columns; on the contrary, they ended up showing me how to use them correctly.

About this time, the guerrillas attacked an army base and took a hundred soldiers prisoner. The government was weakening rapidly. The church, the country's business and industrial sectors, the media, and, of course, the United States united against Samper and he seemed ready to fall. I continued to suggest the country's problems would not be solved by weakening the government but, instead, by initiating peace negotiations. And I insisted the biggest obstacle in the way was the military's refusal to obey civilian power for it was in that breach that the paramilitaries were becoming stronger. My articles became more critical, especially concerning the paramilitaries who continued to massacre campesinos, burn down villages, and selectively murder human rights defenders—all crimes committed with absolute impunity. I then began to receive signed death threats.

I got the first after publishing a column in *El Espectador* about the nature of paramilitarism and its ties to drug traffickers, large landowners, and members of the Colombian army. It called me a "paraguerrilla" in the following terms: "If guerrillas don't respect members of right-wing political parties, we won't respect subversives ensconced in government jobs." That note made me realize how serious the situation had become and made it clear I'd struck some very sensitive nerves. My enemies were reading and paying attention to what I was writing, and I felt they'd drawn a line in the sand.

I ignored it, however, and, in spite of the difficulties, resumed my travels around the country. Listening to people and learning of their problems, which, by this time, had become tragedies, in particular the (at that time) one million campesinos who had been displaced by terror. I was hurt deeply by the killings of conservationist friends of mine with whom I'd tried to defend the *páramos,* the jungles, and the rivers from the greed of cattle ranchers and to denounce the lethal consequences of fumigating illegal crops; of lawyers who had taken on human rights cases; of Indians who'd been murdered for demanding respect for their land and traditions; and of journalists, who investigated enforced disappearances, kidnappings, and massacres. I wrote a column in which, in spite of my fear, I said: "The time has come to tell the country about the ties between the establishment, the State, and the paramilitaries and to do away with everything that stands in the way of the exercise of democracy and a civilian opposition. Everything that is happening scares us. And writing about it scares us even more. But it is a fear we have to live with."

When the threats against me became public, the commander

of the army called me to his office and offered me protection. He told his men to come up with a list of security measures I needed to implement in order to stay alive. After visiting me at home, they concluded I had to start by cutting down all the trees around my house. Then, I had to install reflectors, alarms, and a sentry-post, hire some around-the-clock bodyguards, and begin using a bulletproof car. It goes without saying the government wouldn't be paying for any of these measures.

Several months later, after the new administration had taken office, I wrote that President Pastrana, in spite of his good intentions, would not be able to advance in his quest for peace until he dealt unequivocally with the paramilitaries. And I warned that, should he do so, he ran the risk of dividing the armed forces because it was inexplicable how the paramilitaries could continue to act with the impunity they did. Before I had even submitted the article, I received a present: *The Black Book of Communism*, a well-known investigative report written by a team from the Paris-based National Scientific Research Center (CNRS), with a somewhat cryptic, handwritten dedication: "History has a special place reserved for those who write it and another for those who distort it." Three days later, I got another message telling me the paramilitaries could not be "dismantled" as I had insisted they should be. But what could be done—and they were going to do it, the message said—was dismantle the "paraguerrilla," which had done more harm to the country's institutions than the guerrillas themselves. In its editorial, *El Espectador* responded to this: "The objective of the self-defense groups is to silence the voices that criticize them and achieve political recognition in order to gain access to the negotiating table." The paramilitaries were quick to answer: "We have irrefutable proof that Mr.

Molano is a member of the parasubversion, is not an enemy of the self-defense groups but of the nation, and is an intellectual sniper, prejudiced in his judgements and biased in his analysis." They ended by saying: "Mr. Director, we would like to publicly reiterate our respect for free speech, criticism, and dissent."

That same night, December 24, I decided to go into exile. The Spanish embassy in Colombia had offered me protection and the possibility of establishing myself in Spain. Although I'd thought about leaving the country since receiving the first threat, it's difficult to know exactly what made up my mind for me. I felt the danger, although I'd done what I could to hide it, and knew that leaving would mean distancing myself from my children, my friends, and from all the other things a person accumulates and comes to love: a horse, a book, a pair of running shoes. The look in some of my friends' eyes, however, told me that they, too, felt threatened when they were with me. And when, on seeing me again, one or another of them would say: "What? You're still alive?" I knew that was that. I had nothing left inside me to respond to a new and offensive letter which arrived, this time unsigned: "The sooner they bury you the better. If you're a communist, you're a bandit and that's the same as being a terrorist, you son-of-a-bitch. Wherever you are, the *autodefensas* will come for you."

The next day, without saying goodbye to my children because I am a weak man, I boarded a plane to Spain. I took only a few shirts and some books with me because I didn't want to put down roots anywhere far from my country. I never want to feel like a stranger here. In spite of all the pain it entails, exile has taught me to look the loneliness that is always with me straight in the eye and to possess no more than the clothes I am wearing so that, at any time or on any day, I'll be free to return to Colombia. The bitter tastes of being far from home change and sometimes become almost bittersweet although there is an oppressive weight I drag along with me from street to street and from night to night. During the first days of my exile, I couldn't help but think I was the same little boy who my parents left in the care of one of their lady friends one day, and who, for lunch, began to gobble down sausages so voraciously that it made me squeeze my legs together.

I arrived in Barcelona and found a dark apartment, depressing in the long, grey winter days. I went out only to buy the food I needed, returning to write, and, above all, to use the telephone. I lived forty-eight-hour days, twenty-four in Colombia and twenty-four in Spain. With the first flowers on the cherry trees, life returned to Barceloneta, my barrio, and one morning at dawn, the silence was broken by a cacophony of trumpets and drums. That night everyone dressed in costumes—as fish, tigers, clowns, vampires—and went to the Plaza San Miguel where there was a *vacaloca* and fireworks. I wasn't in the mood for parties, though, and went instead to the ocean, the cold ocean— a contradiction I will never get used to—and let it carry me away as the rivers used to do when I was a boy.

The routes you plan out and follow each day in exile are narrow ones. You have the same fear of the abyss the ancient sailors had, a fear that shuts you in and imposes an unbearable redundancy on your steps. I am sure it's the same sensation *colonos* feel alone on the mountainside before they begin to dominate it, little by little, with their machetes as they clear the land to plant and, above all, gain a view of the distance so they can see who is coming. Like the colonos, I began to "find myself" and make

peace with the walls of my apartment, with the street corners
of my barrio, and the streets of Barcelona, until I realized
they had never declared war on me.

Then, one afternoon, I felt the urge to eat bananas—
even if they weren't from Urabá—and to buy African yucca
and some *granadillas* from Urrao that I'd seen in a store
selling exotic products. I've never been very patriotic, at least
not like Señor Caro, who for having spent all his time translating Virgil* never saw the Magdalena River, but now, from
afar, I must confess that I began to find even *bambucos*
appealing. I missed my friends and my travels across the
cordilleras and the *llanos*. I even began to miss my enemies.
You have to learn to distinguish between the country, as land
and as home, and the political system that has it in the state
it is. After repeated efforts to strike up a conversation, sometimes with no answer at all, the barber from the corner and
the baker began to talk to me. It was difficult for us to
understand each other. To many people, Colombians speak
an old-fashioned Spanish, which makes it difficult to guess
where we learned it. But the Spaniards, the fine Spanish
people, are cheerful, they drink clean wine, take siestas, and
haven't forgotten the gunpowder taste of the lentils they
were forced to eat during the terrible Spanish civil war.

Come what may, I will not repeat the history of the
Spanish republicans or the Chileans and Argentinians who
left saying they'd be back in two weeks and returned—those

---

* Annibal Caro was the sixteenth-century Italian translator of Virgil's *Aeneid*, the
classical Roman epic poem. In translating the *Aeneid* from Latin into vernacular
Italian, Caro intended to promote a sense of patriotism for early modern Rome
rooted in the "glories" of the Roman Empire.

of them who did return—thirty years later. Washing my underwear in the sink and watching the specks of dust that inhabit old cities float through the sunlit air of my apartment, I have composed love poems in my head that I'll never write down; passionate discourses against paramilitary crimes and their complicity with the army and police—which I will publish someday; and long and tedious essays with French sociologists and their épigones about the significance of civil society. I won't say I have re-thought the country. But I have come to understand its importance, its very minimal importance, to people in these cold latitudes. To Europeans, for example, *La Virgen de los Sicarios,* that marvelous movie of that marvelous book, is considered as far-fetched and unbelievable, although not nearly as amusing, as *Charlie's Angels.* And there is only a small chance that anything thoughtful about Colombia, other than the usual drivel about blood and coca, will be published in the newspapers in Spain, especially when so much space is given to the pop singer Rocio Jurado's stupid love affair with her bullfighter husband who isn't even a bullfighter anymore.

Writing about our realities from here is difficult. It means not only daring to acknowledge them—a daily and always painful exercise—but also doing it without living and breathing them. When I read and re-read what I write, it seems dry and full of those traps the magic of words makes it so easy to fall into. But writing about the realities of Europe is even more difficult because almost none of them resonate in the hell that our country has become. How important can Spain's Hydrological Plan be to me when I know fifty campesinos were killed with machetes by paramilitaries in Chengue? I read the debates about the plan and it's like they're talking about some micro-organic fossils that were found a hundred years ago on a meteorite that fell from Mars. Of course, there is news that affects us—the mad cows, the reemergence of racism, and even the future of Barca (the Barcelona soccer team)—but the only news that really means anything to me is that which touches on the solution to our war.

I am convinced that a negotiated solution to the country's armed conflict—even in the midst of all its ills—is a life or death proposition for me because, apart from meting out justice to people who've always been excluded, it is my only hope of going back to Colombia and being able to live without all those shields, which are as hostile as they are useless. It's my only chance of once again being able to walk along remote country paths without having to look constantly over my shoulder, and, most of all, my only chance of being able to see my grandson grow up. I will never get used to being in exile although, today, I know that small death begins not with the threats of your enemies but with the silence of your friends.

When they murdered Jaime Garzón,* however, I knew I could not go home soon. So I picked out a large work table, sharpened my pencil, and began this book. On completing it, I understood—and bowed my head in profound respect—that in spite of its pains, the drama of my exile is but a pale reflection of the terrible tragedy that millions of Colombians live each day, uprooted and exiled in their own country. I believe, as they do, that the seeds of a true democracy can be found only in a negotiated political agreement. The war will have only one outcome, the dictatorship of the victors.

---

* Jaime Garzón, a journalist and human rights advocate, was Colombia's best-loved political satirist. Assassins gunned him down on a Bogotá street in August, 1999.

Chapter 2

The Defeat

I watched her spread her things out on the bed, the way we always did, then open her bag and pack quickly. She left without looking at me. I had known she no longer loved me since the day we stopped laughing together. But I didn't dwell on it, so I wouldn't have to believe it and accept it. I was expecting this farewell, and I reminded her of that the day she came back distraught and told me what had happened. She knew I had to write about her in order to put a period—or perhaps a semicolon—after my grief.

Boca del Cajambre is a port hidden in a mangrove swamp on Colombia's Pacific coast. Or at least in what the negro Bonifacio Mosquera left of the mangrove after building a house, buying a boat, bringing up a family there, and setting up a sawmill, which he kept going by selling "illegal woods" like mangrove to Don Enrique Ortiz, a businessman who bought all the wood he could get his hands on to sell to Cartones Colombianos.* It was finding out about that little business that proved to be the beginning of the end for Diego and his friend Aníbal. Someone in Buenaventura had told them about the settlement of whites being organized along the Cajambre River and the two old men had been their neighbors since she and her boyfriend arrived. That had been her dream ever since I first met her—to live by the ocean with nothing more than the sarong she was wearing. Even if that meant supporting Ramón from time to time as I assumed it would.

Diego was a petroleum engineer who'd spent all his life working for Ecopetrol. After finishing school in the Escuela de Minas in Medellín, he was put in charge of the Puerto Niño camp in the Middle Magdalena River valley during the 1950s. After that, he moved to El Tarra in Norte de Santander to run the company's operations, then went to Kuwait to take a lengthy course. He retired after that and, to make life easier for his wife and children, bought the house they'd been renting, then left for Boca del Cajambre. There, he built a small house beside the ocean and spent his time learning to play chess with a book he'd bought in Istanbul about the great chess masters, from Capablanca to Kasparov.

---

* Colombian subsidiary of Irish pulp and paper multinational, Jefferson Smurfit.

One morning, Diego saw a man land on the beach. He had a white beard and carried a backpack and Diego thought he was probably a traveler passing through. But that wasn't the case. He'd come to stay, and, for that reason, Diego resolved not to help him. Not a word passed between the two men for six months. Then one afternoon, Aníbal—that was the old man's name—walked over from the house he had built and challenged Diego to a game of chess. Even though Diego lost the game, it helped him become friends with the man he nicknamed "el forastero," the outsider.

Aníbal had been a chauffeur for the Mallarinos, an ill-tempered aristocratic family from Bogotá. When his wife died, he decided to spend his time fishing, a passion of his since his boss, Don Arturo, introduced him to its solitary pleasures on his way back from a trip to Florida. Aníbal knew every intimate detail of the Mallarinos' political and amorous intrigues, and he reproached himself for being unable to write about them in order to tell the country what these so-called decent people were really made of. Instead of writing, he watched the ocean, his small blue eyes glued to his spyglass.

The old men became good friends. They played chess each afternoon and ate the fish Aníbal caught every morning while Diego tended the garden which, to be fair, was only four yucca plants, two papachina roots, and a couple of plantains. The men had few needs. Diego took care of an emaciated cat that had appeared one night, and Aníbal made regular visits to a black woman, generous of her laughter and her body and happy to trade both for a couple of bottles of *biche,* a local *aguardiente* very popular in the region. You could say the two men were living out their golden years in a well-deserved and serene manner.

Their only concern was the destruction of the mangroves, and both men had gone to Buenaventura and Cali to tell the authorities about it. But Don Enrique, the biggest buyer, had influential political friends and had put up an impenetrable wall around his business with the votes Bonifacio Mosquera brought him from the men who cut the "illegal" wood and then brazenly stacked it in the port. There were many of them because there was mangrove a long way up the Cajambre River and because Mosquera exploited not only the Cajambre, but also the Agua Sucia, Timba, and Yarumanguí Rivers as well.

One day, the men heard that Don Enrique had been kidnapped.

"It must have been the guerrillas," said Diego.

"Don't forget, there are also common criminals," replied Aníbal.

No one ever found out who paid the ransom, and the wood business continued, with the cutting increased to make up for what had been paid to the kidnappers.

It was about this time that María José—that was her name—and her companion arrived in Boca del Cajambre. They built a shack, hung their hammocks, and dug a fire pit where they could grill their fish. That was all she wanted, and it didn't take long for the new arrivals and the old men to become friends. Neither bothered the other, and a mutual respect soon existed between them. Then, one afternoon, she saw a group of armed men get out of their boats and come ashore. "Strange, the army coming all the way out here," she thought as she called Ramón.

There were fifteen men and four women. They walked over to the shack and, without any small talk, said they were guerrillas. They'd be seeing a lot of them from now on, they added, and then, in a severe tone, warned them that the only thing they wouldn't tolerate were informants. *Sapos,* they called them. Before they left, the guerrillas also visited Diego and Aníbal.

Days passed and no one saw or heard from them again. But everyone knew they were still around, showing up from time to time, then turning around and disappearing from where they'd come.

The guerrillas came back at about ten in the morning on December 24. Just five of them, four men and a girl. Aníbal was out fishing and Diego was preparing a *natilla* for Christmas Eve. They sat down and began talking to Diego. The guerrilla commander recalled how people prepared stuffed pig at Christmastime in El Espinal, his hometown. By the time Aníbal arrived, the conversation had become lively, and he sliced up the fish he'd caught and offered it to the guerrillas with some biche. While the men ate, a guerrillera asked if instead of a glass of aguardiente, she could take a shower. Aníbal, a lady's man, was glad to be of help and got her a towel, some soap, and shampoo. By the time she'd left the bathroom, picked up her things, and packed them in her Hello Kitty backpack, the men had finished off half a bottle of biche. Aníbal told her the shower would be available anytime she wanted it.

"And so will he," added Diego with a smile.

In spite of Aníbal's insistence they continue the Christmas Eve celebration, the guerrillas left when the bottle was finished. Everyone else stayed up until dawn drinking. When María José awoke on Christmas morning, she sensed something bad had happened during the night. But no one said anything or had any complaints, and she concluded the sensation was simply a result of drinking too much.

The feeling stayed with her the next day though and throughout the week. Ramón said maybe it was because she'd been taken with the guerrilla commander, and Mariá José, who has a temper, told him to eat shit, saying he was the one who was "keeping" another woman in Buenaventura. Aníbal's lady friend had told her that and María José—I know her well—was spoiling for a fight.

María José didn't sleep well on January 7. She tossed and turned in the hammock and woke up several times during the night. The silence was absolute, and, except for the ocean, there was no sound at all. Early the next morning, Aníbal arrived and told her he'd found the dogs dead. They'd been poisoned, he said, and had their snouts covered with slobber. María José told me later it was at that moment she knew they all had to get away from Boca del Cajambre.

The next morning, Diego came running up like a crazy man, crying for help and saying they'd killed Aníbal. When he calmed down, he told them a group of men with guns had arrived at about nine the night before. Taking them for guerrillas, Aníbal greeted them politely. He then realized his mistake.

"You are a guerrilla son-of-a-bitch," said the one in charge. "And we've come to pay you back for your partying with those bandits." Without another word, he pulled out a pistol and shot Aníbal three times in the face.

Aníbal spun sideways and fell onto the book María José had given him for Christmas, *Daughter of Fortune* by Isabel Allende. Diego was petrified. The killer looked at him and said:

"As for you, you little bastard, I won't kill you. But only so you can tell everyone what happened. I don't want the flies eating both of you before they find out Lieutenant Aguirre from the Death Squad is here, cleaning up guerrillas from the region."

He hit Diego, threw him down on the ground, and kicked him a couple of times in the ribs. Paralyzed with fear, he lay there motionless waiting for the dawn.

María José and her companion ran to Aníbal's house. They found him lying on the floor in a pool of blood, the flies circling his body.

María José ran out of the house and on to Puerto Caraña, the closest town, for help. She went straight to the police station. When she got there, the police chief told her calmly: "We already know about it. But we have orders not to leave here. Bring the old man's body here and we'll take care of it."

On she went, crying, to the priest's house.

"Look, I can't bring that kind of body into the church. And, anyway, you must know the Three Wise Men arrive today," he told her.

Disconsolate, María José began to walk aimlessly through the town. Behind closed doors and windows, people asked each other: *"Is it true? What did they do to him? How many times did they shoot him? Do you think he was the compañera's boyfriend?"*

María José felt as if she were losing her mind. Finally, she ran into Celestino, the village idiot, a man who passed the time carving crosses for "repentant sinners" on mangrove trees and building altars on the town's streets to "cleanse the air."

When he saw María José, he said, "I'll sing Don Aníbal's praises to the Lord."

Later that afternoon, Ramón and Diego arrived carrying the old man's body. No one would let them into their house for the wake, and they couldn't find a coffin anywhere in town. So they ended up laying the body on a pool table in a bar called The Ace of Hearts.

Celestino sung his praises through the night while Diego and Ramón got drunk. When it got light enough, the two men dragged the body down to the water, lifted it onto a boat and, when they were far enough offshore, threw it into the water. Back on shore, María José left Celestino singing, and, without turning around to look at Ramón, walked out of the town.

She arrived from Cali last night and hasn't stopped crying since. She is beside me now as I write.

Chapter 3

Ángela*

I never wore shoes in Nechí. We all went barefoot—my brothers and sisters, my cousins, and almost everyone else in town. We didn't need shoes because everything on the ground there is either sand or mud. Even after I got blisters on the bottom of my feet and my feet got soft, I didn't need shoes. I liked to walk barefoot in the barrio, and I never got sick like some people say you will if you don't wear shoes.

We lived in a barrio called Pueblo Nuevo.

* Interviewed by Natalia Peña

It's on a small hill, so there was no mud there, only sand, and, when the sun heated it up, you had to walk fast and try to keep your feet off the ground, so you wouldn't burn them. When it rained a lot, the river overflowed into the street, leaving every- thing muddy. That's when we liked to go out, slipping and sliding along on the soft mud before the sun hardened it, or the wind turned it into dust.

I had two changes of clothes in Nechí. I'd put one on while the other was being washed. When it was dry, I'd change again. It all depended on the weather. When it was sunny and hot, I'd change quickly. If not, I'd wear the same clothes until it stopped raining. My three younger brothers and sisters had the same rou- tine. The difference was they'd use the clothes I had already worn.

I had a baby brother and sister in Nechí, and neither one liked me. My sister didn't like me because she had to wear my hand-me-downs and my brother didn't like me because he had to wear girl's clothes, and the kids at school used to ask him if he had to wear my underwear as well.

My father, Rafael, gave us everything we needed at home, and my mother took care of us. My father fished and drove the *yonson,* the motorboat, on the river. Other times, he helped unload boats and worked as a messenger. And when times were really tough, he'd sell ice cream cones for a man who paid him commission. That was the job I liked best because when I'd go into town looking for him, he'd give me a free cone, even though it would be taken off his pay. I liked coconut cones the most because they had a kind of fiber in them that made you want to suck on them hard to get all their taste. But my father didn't like the job much and said that when it was hot, most of the money he made melted inside the pail he carried the ice cream in.

My father spoiled me and called me his angel. My older
sister died when she was two, a little before I was born. Someone
put the evil eye on her. My father named me Ángela (Angel), so
he wouldn't go crazy, and so I could watch over him. My grandparents gave me my second name, María. My grandmother said
her oldest granddaughter had to have that name, and, since my
sister who died was named María, it was up to me to have the
name too. My father gave us tiger tooth bracelets to wear so that
what happened to my sister wouldn't happen to us. I don't understand about the "evil eye" being put on a child, but it scares me
because when children die as children, it's because of the evil eye.
I don't know who would look at you that way. I look into the
eyes of the old women to see if they're evil, but I don't see it.
And I haven't seen it in the eyes of the men here either. I don't
know where it comes from or who carries it or what pleasure they
get from killing children. They say they are souls that belong to
someone else and live in people they shouldn't.

I went to school in Nechí and learned to read and write, to
count, and to sing and play. I finished grade two and always
ended up at the top of my class. What I didn't like about getting
the highest marks was that I had to raise the flag in the morning.
And that I had to climb up on a bench to reach the string I pulled
to make the flag—or what the teacher called the national tri-
color—go up the pole. I'd rather play with my father. He taught
me to play games, and that's better than learning how to pray.

Sometimes, he'd pretend he was a horse. All three of us kids
would climb on him and when he said "*Arre,*" off he'd go running,
then galloping with us holding on until we all ended up on the
ground in a pile. Other times, we'd all run in the street in front
of our house. It was a long street, and we'd run down it with a

sad-looking dog with long, droopy ears named Lauro. He was nine, the same age as me, and had an expression on his face like a child who had been scolded. We'd yell "*Usi, usi,*" and he'd take off with us running down the street behind him. Lauro took care of us and made sure no strangers got near the house. When they did, he'd bark and even bite. We had a cat too. We never gave it a name. Whenever my father saw it trying to get out he'd grab it by the tail, and it'd meow and meow. That would make my mother laugh, and we'd all feel happy. I liked Lauro the most. I'd tickle him with my bare feet, and we'd both feel good. We liked each other.

I had a lot of friends. Almost all of them were my cousins. My best friend was my Aunt Sofia, who was also about nine. We used to play "cinco huecos," which is a man's game. You draw a big square on the street and then other, smaller squares inside it. Because my name is Angela, I'd put an "A" in one of the smaller squares. Then you'd turn around and throw a little stick over your head. If it landed on your letter, you had to get the others out by hitting them with a ball. I liked that game. It was fun, but sometimes men on motorcycles would drive over the squares and ruin the game with their tires and their boots. We couldn't say anything to them or even look at them like we were mad because our fathers told us they were from the paramilitary, and, when they got mad, they killed people. I never saw their guns because they were small, and they kept them hidden in their backpacks. But all the adults were afraid of them. My father told me not to ask them for anything or to mention them at all. He also told me never to talk about the guerrillas or go to evangelical meetings. I used to like their meetings because they sang and sang all day long. Sometimes, I'd stand listening to them and hours would pass by with me there crouched down by the door. No one in our family ever went to the Catholic church. The priest was a grouch, and we didn't like the way he smelled like dead flowers.

When we weren't at school, which was most of the time because the teacher said she wouldn't be back until she'd been paid, we'd go to the beach along the river. The breeze and the water would cool us off. My grandfather taught me to fish with a locked hook, like my grandmother's earrings, which was a kind of trap you baited with the guts of the first fish you caught. We caught a lot of *barbudos* because they're such gluttons and so greedy they eat everything they see in front of them. Once I caught a big one, a huge one, so big that we made a *sancocho* that fed all of us with some left over for Lauro and the cat. My father got angry when he saw me come home with that fish because he thought I'd stolen it. A child doesn't catch a fish that big, he said. And if he does hook it, he doesn't try to land it.

We used to go down to the river a lot to cool off, especially in the afternoon, until my father forbade it because of the bodies that began to float by. He didn't want us to see them. I never saw a dead body in the river, but I used to hear people saying the river was full of them. I didn't mind if the river was full of bodies because then my father would take us to some clear streams where there were small, colored fish that came up to bite your toes and tickle you with their tiny mouths when you put your feet in the water. I used to take them bits of rice, and they'd stir up the water so much they looked like tiny lights. We tried to catch some of them in a handkerchief so as not to hurt them, but we never managed to hold one in our hands.

Once, when we were with my father taking some wood along the river, a group of men called to us from shore. They wore uniforms like the police, but they weren't policemen because they didn't have clubs hanging from their belts but carried big rifles instead. My father steered the boat toward them to hear what they wanted. They asked if he'd take them across the river. We did because, as my dad said, when men have guns, it's not a favor they ask you for, and you have no choice but to do it.

After that, the man who owned the *yonson* told my father he couldn't work on the river anymore because the paramilitaries were furious when they found out the men we took across the river were guerrillas. But my father didn't know who they were. No one told me that, but I overheard a man telling my father about it, and, later, when he told my mother what happened, she got very scared.

My father couldn't go back to the river and that was the end of our trips in the *yonson*. He began selling ice cream and piling crates in a store. My grandfather gave me some lottery tickets to sell with an aunt who was older than me. I spent everything I earned on bread. It was something I really loved to eat. I also helped my mother take care of my baby brother. He was always trying to get out of the house and into the street, and sometimes we had to be very stern with him.

When he got some time before or after work, my father would work on the house he was building for us. He'd been working on it for years so that we could stop paying rent. First he bought a small yard and cleaned it up. Then, brick by brick, he built one wall and then another. He'd buy a cheap block of cement whenever he could, and every week or so, we'd help him by bringing the water to mix and he'd add it on. He finished the big room first, and we all moved in there to live. Then he started on the kitchen. He finished the living room next and put a floor down and made doors. We had a garden that ran all the way around the house and flowers in the front and back, and I planted green beans, real ones, not like the ones we've had to plant here in Bogotá, all shriveled up and dry.

Everything grew well in the garden: *ají*, tomatoes, lemon, papaya, and yucca, and there was enough for all of us to eat and sometimes enough to give the neighbors. When we had them all picked, it was like our house was a store with people from all over coming in to buy one thing or another. In Nechí, it was just a matter of reaching your hand out and picking something to eat. There was a yellow fruit called *anón cienaguero,* and, when it ripened, you didn't even have to put out your hand to pick it because it fell all by itself. When my uncle Ulises came by the house and saw it, he'd say to my mother, "Listen, Carmen, I'll trade you my life for one of those anónes."

It made me feel a little funny, wondering what my mother would do with two lives. It was such a delicious fruit, we'd all look for it and try to keep it from falling out of the tree, so it wouldn't break open.

Something else you don't see here in Bogotá is sugar cane. Sometimes my father would arrive with fresh grass for his donkey and sugar cane for us. He'd cut it up, and we'd get in line for the pieces that were left over. You had to suck them hard to get all that sweet tasty juice they had. Even my mother would line up with a glass in her hand to get some of it. Boy, do I miss that sugar cane! I haven't tasted it since or even seen it here, just like I haven't eaten any more fish. I only eat meat here in Bogotá. Well, really just bones because the meat is too expensive, and there's never enough money to buy it. I miss the meat from the wild animals we used to eat: the *guatinaja* and the armadillo my father used to bring back from the hills where he went shellfishing. He'd always come back with his shirt soaked with sweat but never with his hands empty.

Here in Bogotá, my mother gives us *agua de panela* and *arepa* for breakfast. For lunch, rice and potatoes, and for supper, rice. We almost never get plantains. At home, we drank the liquid from cheese curd when we got tired of eating fish, and, when my father got tired of eating guatinaja, he'd kill a turtle. I'd help him by pulling on the head and feet. You can only get meat from turtles like that when they're alive because, if you kill them without removing their shells first, they shrivel up and hide all their meat.

You have to flip them over, belly up, and pry away with a knife until you get the shell off. Without its shell, a turtle looks like a newborn bird, all wrinkled up and lost even though it's still alive. You have to be careful of your fingers, though, because it can bite them right off. I'd put a stick in its mouth for it to get mad at and bite instead. You have to cut off the feet and pull off all the meat while it's still alive until you finally cut off the head. We liked turtle the most when it was all mixed up in a stew, because that way we couldn't tell which part was which.

After my father stopped going down to the river, our electricity was cut off. We didn't have enough money to pay for it anymore. I didn't mind that because it meant we could all go down to the beach when the heat became too stifling in the house. We didn't have a fan to get the heat out into the street. But it made my father sad. He liked to lean his stool back against the wall and watch television while my mother cooked. So we'd go with my grandfather instead, but only if he was sure there were no bodies floating in the river that day. If there were, they'd shut us in the house before the sun went down to swat at the mosquitoes.

My mother would get all four of us into the mosquito netting. But it had to be stretched tightly, so they wouldn't find a way through it, and we couldn't get to sleep for the heat. I'd cry a lot because of that and ask my mother to put a sheet over the mattress to cool it off.

Everybody was inside by eight o'clock. The adults would sit outside talking among themselves until then, because later, the paramilitaries would ride by on their motorcycles and kill whoever wasn't inside. It was scary seeing all the streets empty and all the people afraid. Whenever there were bodies in the river, the paramilitaries showed up. We were all inside the house by then. My father gave me some baby chicks, so I wouldn't be so bothered by the heat. I took care of them and tried to fatten them up, but we had a lot of rats in the house, and they hunted at night, so I tried my best not to go to sleep, so I could keep an eye on the chicks.

One night I woke up, not because of the chicks, but because of some shots I heard in the street. They were so loud and seemed so close we thought they'd hit somewhere in the house—even louder at night with the echo the street seems to have. My mother began to cry and say they were going to kill us, and I ran out to count my chicks and make sure they were all right. But they were all dead, suffocated in the can. I'd shut the lid too tight to try and keep the rats out. My father looked at the dead chicks there and said to my mother he was afraid the same thing was going to happen to us. He'd been afraid since the night they turned our electricity off, the same night a young man was found dead in the middle of town. My father told us his tongue had been cut out and that pieces of his fingers had been cut off, like we used to do to the turtles. He tried to console my mother by saying it would be the last person the paramilitaries killed there because the authorities had told them not to kill anybody else inside the town. My father said that now they'd have to take the people they were going to kill out of town, far away, where the families wouldn't find them. I didn't see the man's body but I heard everything my father told my mother about him.

My youngest sister was born in the house we built with my father. The rest of us were born in houses that weren't ours. My sister was lucky because she was born in something that was hers. My father came home one afternoon with the midwife, and my mother told us we were going to have another member of the family. I don't think it hurt because she didn't cry out or say anything at all. They sent all the kids outside, but I wanted to know what was going on. My aunt Mariela saw me standing by the bedroom door, though, and sent me out too, so I didn't see anything. Just a tiny baby wrapped in a towel, a little bundle they said was named Leidy. My father calmed down when they showed her to him, squirming around like a little lizard.

I think he loves us all a lot. He treats us well and doesn't argue with my mother very much. One thing he has never liked is children hearing what the adults talk about. He says when they hear those things and talk about them, they get their parents into trouble. I overheard him telling my mother in secret that he was going to have to leave because they'd told him to leave. I don't know who it was that told him that, but, a couple of days later, we found Lauro dead in the street. He'd been poisoned. My father was furious, saying the people who had become his enemies had done it, but my mother said the men who were his enemies didn't kill animals. I know my father was afraid of the paramilitaries, of those men who kill and kill. One day I asked him why he was going away and leaving us, and he said he had no choice. I asked him again another time, and he told me that he had to go until he got tired and told me to stop asking so much. But I knew he had to go because of those men who hated him, the ones who killed Lauro. I didn't ask him again, but I got very sad the night he left for Bogotá.

My mother cried ever day after that because she felt alone, and I cried when I saw her crying. We were both probably thinking he would never come back. There were a lot of kids in town with no father; some had gone away with other women, others, like ours, had been forced to leave or had been killed. I didn't want to be without my father, and, when he left, I started to feel hungry day and night. All of us did. My mother had to start washing people's clothes. There are rich people in Nechí who dirty a lot of clothes, and that was good for my mother because it meant she had more work to do. She came home each afternoon with three thousand pesos, and we spent it all on food to eat. We bought rice and panela in town, and my grandfather sent us some fish and sometimes some turtle. But even so, nothing was the same as when my father was with us. Everything was less. He was working here in Bogotá but couldn't send us any money. And since my mother left early and came back late, we ate breakfast but not lunch. Lunches ended when my father went away. We went hungry all day until my mother came back, and we could eat something at night.

That's how we all were the day the river overflowed and flooded the town. We ended up living with everyone else in the town's sports complex. As soon as my father heard what happened, he sent for us because he'd made enough to send us money for tickets. He also sent some socks and some pretty, secondhand shoes, so we could meet him in Bogotá.

It made me sad to leave our house, but I'd do anything to be with my father again, wherever it might be. The shoes were too tight for me, and I arrived in Bogotá carrying them in my hand. He brought us to live here in the south of the city. This house is smaller than the one we had. It has only one room, a bathroom, and the front door. The first night I slept here, I was so cold it felt as if someone had poured ice water on my head. And when I looked out the next morning, the sky was so dark and it was so cold that I couldn't get out from under the covers. It's so cold here! I don't have any friends, and I haven't got a place in school because there are too many kids, and they don't like kids that come from somewhere else. My mother had to stand in line in Usme one day from six in the morning until seven at night. Finally, they felt sorry for her when she said we were displaced and that she didn't even have enough money for the bus ticket home.

My sister Milena has become my best friend and we sleep together on the same mattress. The rest of the children sleep on the other mattress, and my parents in the bed, unless one of us gets in with them during the night. It's just as well. We are all together in one room because that way we keep each other warm and don't freeze to death, and we can keep each other company. What I like about Bogotá is the television because it's in color. In Nechí, it was black and white. I go to bed at ten but I start warming up my spot on the mattress at eight.

We have everything we need because my father has a job carrying bricks at a construction site. He goes to work at four in the morning and comes back at nine at night. That's why we eat every day, and, when there's extra money, he buys us things. He promised me some red running shoes, like the ones the mouse on television wears. I think he's going to get them for me as a present. The shoes I have are too tight and my sister uses them now. I cry when I have to put them on. I almost never cried in Nechí, only when I'd fall down and skin my knee. And sometimes I cry here because I'm afraid of the *gamines*, because they rob you. There aren't any gamines in Nechí, and, if someone is caught stealing, all the neighbors give him a beating and send him on his way.

It's not the same here. The gamines carry knives and stab the people they steal from. My mother doesn't let us go outside, just as far as the door, because she's afraid of the thieves and the cars. I think it was easier to get food in Nechí, but more difficult to get clothes and shoes. We can get clothes and shoes here, but food costs a lot. My mother can't help my father because she's scared to leave us alone with so many bad things outside in the street.

My mother sent me to the store the other day to buy some yucca, and I got scared when the police arrived on motorcycles and drove right into the store like the paramilitaries used to do in Nechí. My father wants to go back to Nechí because he's afraid we'll lose the house and because he says everything is going to be more difficult here. He says a lot of people like us are arriving with no jobs and no food. But I don't want to go back. If we go back, I'll never get the red running shoes my father promised me.

Chapter 4

Silences

We were just coming into Pinillos when we heard the bombs exploding. The helicopters were coming down out of the sky in a line like hawks, dropping their eggs all at once as if they were at war with everybody. They passed close over our heads, their propellers blowing up a tremendous gust of wind. When I saw they were from the army brigade, I figured the guerrillas had attacked the town. I told La Mona not to worry, that nothing would happen to us because we hadn't done anything. Then, as if they had heard me, the helicopters moved away and started bombing in the swampy area behind the town.

It didn't surprise me the guerrillas had chosen that way out of town and into the hills. They'd done it before. Then we heard the shooting pick up in the town's plaza, and the real battle began.

We continued on down the river close to the shore with the motor turned off, pulling the boat along and staying out of sight. When we reached a clearing, we could see the pier and how the police were dug in, firing toward the river even though most of the shooting was coming from the center of town. I told La Mona that it seemed strange because there was no one there except civilians. Whenever the guerrillas attacked the police station— and they attacked it often—they'd surround it and then fire without stopping at the police until they gave up. But now the police were shooting toward the river.

As we were looking around and wondering what to do next, a girl appeared. She was the girlfriend of one of the town's policemen. As she struggled to catch her breath, she said the *paracos* had come into town at six that morning, shooting at everything that moved. The police had been ordered to stay in their barracks the night before, and the "pests" from the army brigade, as she called them, were firing into the swamp so that no one escaped that way. La Mona knew the girl because they'd worked together at the El Danubio Café in Barranca. She said, "Look, Marina, if that's the case, why don't you go over to the plaza and have a look around. Get us some coffee. We haven't eaten yet today. And come back and tell us what's going on."

A little while later, she came back with coffee and news. Levis was having the people he knew dragged out of their houses, and the paras were tying them up on the ground. Then we heard the worst of it—single shots and silences. Long silences which scared us more than the bombs.

Levis's father was a crafty old man. He'd been a horse thief, and Levis, who is also a bad apple, struck up a friendship with Victor, the guerrilla commander, to protect him. But when people started complaining about Levis, Victor tied him up and paraded him in front of the townspeople until he admitted his crimes and promised to return everything he'd stolen from them. Levis swore vengeance on the guerrillas. He left Pinillos and showed up near Cartagena, in the paras' military training camp, where he prepared for his return. Well, now he'd come back as judge and jury, and everyone he singled out was lying dead in the plaza.

That was the beginning of it. The paracos left and headed toward Loba, and the police began removing the fourteen bodies that lay in the plaza. The army helicopters didn't return that day, and, in town, there was only confusion and fear. A fear that turns eyes away from other eyes and chokes words in the throat before they are spoken.

No one cried at the funeral because Levis was still there. That same day, nine campesinos from Arenal were cut up with chainsaws. After pieces of their bodies were hung up along the roadside, people headed into the hills. They gathered their belongings, their children, and their dogs together and, with what little life they had left in them, fled into the swamps to become invisible.

In spite of what had happened, though, and how it hurt me, I had no intention of going with them. Until La Mona turned to me with a serious expression in her eyes that I knew well and said, "Maybe you can fool them, but you can't fool me." And with that, she gave me a shove off toward the fleeing families.

I caught up with them on the other side of the river in the

Morrocoyal swamp. I grew up around there. My father was born near the town of Cereté when Ana Julia Campos was still alive. As a girl, she heard the stories of abuses committed by politicians and cattle ranchers, and, later, as a woman, she spoke out against the way the bosses of the Berástegui sugar mill treated their workers. My father was with Don Julio Guerra in 1948, when he took up arms around Murrucucú Mountain to avenge the murder of his boss, Jorge Eliécer Gaitán. He was an avowed enemy of the Conservative government of Mariano Ospina Pérez. That long history of fights and bitterness is what tied us to all the other families who fled along the Tiquisio River as we did.

They made shelters out of plastic bags and ceiba branches and put them up on my father's farm. Of course, in those days, he was nobody. That same ceiba tree would prove to be the nail in all our coffins, as my father explained to us that night. The ceiba is a huge tree, ten or fifteen meters tall and at least five meters around its trunk. Ceiba wood is straight and strong, and lumber companies prize it for that, and—more important—because it doesn't warp when it gets wet.

It was the beginning of the end for the jungle when they began cutting it. They used mules to drag the trunks out and the mules needed grass to eat. They turned all that open space into pastureland and then into cattle land. The lumber business financed all the big cattle spreads. They complement each other perfectly, and the loser is always the *colono,* the peasant farmer. Today, the lumber companies around Pinillos have exploited the ceiba to extinction.

It's sad. But it's always been that way. My father was a sawyer, and he also farmed along the San Carlos River, near Montería. When things started going bad and the ranchers began pushing peasants off the land, he figured there was too much virgin land elsewhere for him to end up hanging on some barbed wire. That's what happened to all the workers from Ciénaga de Oro, Rabo Largo, Mateo Gómez, and Bajo Grande who were up in arms fighting for their rights in those days. The police would hang them up on barbed wire as a warning, so they'd back off and go.

So my father packed his things and headed down the Sinú River towards La Doctrina where the Incora [the Colombian Land Reform Institute, ed.] was giving out plots of land. But he got there too late. So on he went, across the Gulf of Urabá and up the Atrato River, by all that beautiful land that spreads out from the shore, until he reached Unguía, the promised land. He settled there up above the old Sautatá hacienda, a lovely piece of land that used to have a sugar mill, huge herds of cattle, and even its own currency.

But it all went bad after the alcohol factory burned down, and, when my old man got there, nothing was left, just the cemetery, the camps where the workers used to live, and the place where the dredge from Barranquilla had run aground. It had been sent to try to pull out the boat that was headed to Valle del Cauca with the machinery the Eder family had bought to set up their sugar mill in Palmira onboard. My father arrived looking for land, and all he really ended up finding were old, broken dreams.

Well, he picked out a piece of land and cleared it with nothing but his hatchet. He used the wood he took off the land to build a house and cleared ten hectares where he planted grass for a small herd of cattle. Eight years later, he had enough put aside to begin improving his spread; four years after that, the government arrived to buy his land. They said they were going to make a national park there.

"National park?" people asked each other. They had no idea what that meant. What ignorance! But it was the government making the offer, and people believed them. Times were different then. The only problem was the farmers had nowhere to go. But the government man, who was as crafty as they come, had the solution: "There's nothing to worry about," he assured them. "The government will put a boat at your disposal, and you can go wherever you want."

And that's what happened. They gave each farmer a check, and then all seventy of them—belongings and all—were taken to the port of Turbo and left there. Well, it took them longer to cash their checks than to buy everything they could get their hands on: clothes, leather boots, motors, revolvers, radios, and, of course, whiskey. Most of them, if not all of them, ran out of money before they'd even spent it. After that, like it says in the Holy Bible, there was only the "gnashing of teeth."

My old man didn't come out of it too badly though. He had some savings and the dream of a farm for his children. There were eight of us in those days, so he just kept on looking for some land. He went back along the Sinú by San Jorge and settled in the Bajo Cauca. He bought a lot and began cutting trees in the Corcovado hills. When he'd made enough money from that, he moved on to a large farm in Achí. The land was half-forested and half-plowed, and he bought it for a good price from a man who was fed up with trudging up and down the mountainside without being able to have any cattle on his land.

We all moved there with him. Working on good land that is debt-free is a pleasure, and we cleared it, put down grass, and cut up the wood almost before we knew it. We all worked together, each one doing what the old man told him to do, according to his age and strength. We named the farm "Gratitude."

We did alright. But we didn't have our own generator or any credit, so we ended up at the mercy of the intermediaries, the middlemen who always have quick fingers and cold hearts. The farms on either side of us were owned by Antioqueños, and they grew quicker than ours. Their pastures were good and rich like their cattle, so well fed it looked like they were about to burst. A poor man never wins a race of pastureland or cattle.

So one day, after mulling it over for a long while and making a trip to Pinillos to unload some of his wood, my father decided to sell out to one of the neighbors and set off with us along the Tiquisio River. He'd been all through there as a sawyer and told us the land and air were "fresher." Fresher, sure, we found out later, but unforgiving. There was nothing but water around Tiquisio in those days.

I was eighteen and becoming a man. We drove steel rods into the ground and built a house over a gully and planted some corn, rice, plantains, and yucca. We called the farm "El Barco." Then we started in again to clear the forest. This time, though, instead of pastureland and cattle like we had in "Gratitude," we decided to try our luck with marijuana. We'd heard about it, as you hear about something that exists far away. Others did well with it though, and, when we saw that growing it didn't change or degrade them, or make them end up killing one another, we decided to give it a try.

At first, everybody made more money from marijuana than they'd ever made from wood or cattle—or even from the gold mines in Santa Rosa del Sur. They made so much money that pretty soon the big ranchers and gold buyers began to pay for the crops. A lot of well-known politicians nowadays started by lending farmers money to grow marijuana and then buying it from them. Growing marijuana made a lot of people rich around here. We were able to buy some chainsaws and a generator with what we'd made and even a plot of land in Pinillos. My father wanted us to learn how to work the land, but he also wanted us to study.

"You have to learn how to read the land, and you can only do that by studying," he'd say to us.

We continued working the farm and brought in some cattle as well. If you knew what you were doing, marijuana seduced you, and everybody thought they'd grabbed a little piece of paradise by growing it. Until one day, it revealed the evil it could bring.

On December 20, my brother went to Pinillos to sell half a ton he'd grown on a piece of land my father gave him for being the oldest. He was paid in bundles of two thousand peso notes. Five hundred peso notes had been taken out of circulation because the police were trying to track down thieves who'd robbed a stack of them from a bank in Nariño. That made each bundle of bills he took with him even more attractive to the men who killed him. They were hired killers, *sicarios*, and we all knew they worked for the same people who bought the marijuana.

It was a cruel killing. My brother got his money between ten and eleven in the morning and went into a bar for a drink to celebrate the deal. He had a beer. He was never much of a drinker, especially with all that money in his pocket, and they got him in the port.

They found his body three days later, covered with some sacks under a boat that was being caulked. That was the beginning of the end for my father. He lost his will to live after that and left everything in our hands.

When you work without a boss, you get in a lot of arguments. And when you're young, you want to have your own money and be able to spend it anyway you want, without owing anyone an explanation. That's why I decided to leave and go to work in the banana plantations. I went away, far away, and was hired on a plantation in Chigorodó. I cut bananas all day in that heat with the smell of poison in the air and with a man with a gun watching me.

The union had negotiated for eight hours and that's what we worked. But eight hours with a quota. We had to cut a minimum number of bunches an hour or, in my case, hang them up on the cable.

The quota hadn't been agreed on, though, and wasn't in our contract, so we went on strike. The farm boss called in the army, and the army captain accused us of sympathizing with the guerrillas and threatened to "punish us." But our union leaders stood up to him, and the captain, without saying anything to us, simply turned and walked away. A couple of days later, we were starting work in the morning when I saw what looked like some banana bunches wrapped in black plastic hanging on the cable. That seemed strange to me because we didn't use those kinds of bags and hadn't left any bunches there.

Well, when I went to have a closer look, I almost passed out. It was the president and the secretary of the union hanging there. I didn't think twice. I just turned around and got out of there. Thinking back now and without wanting to offend anyone, I think those killings saved a lot of lives because almost all the workers left the plantations after that to get away from working in that hell. No one was ever punished for those murders, and the bosses never lost as much as a minute's sleep over them.

I went back to Tiquisio. La Mona was less a girl and more of a

woman now, in spite of the fact that I'd only been in Chigorodó
for a year and a half. I think there are times when stages of your
life fly by rather than just pass by, and, in my absence, La Mona
had learned to run boats on the river and had grown into a
pretty, happy young woman. When I'd look at her sitting in the
boat with her hair blowing backwards in the wind, I'd feel like
we were in a dream together, and, without saying anything to
her, I knew I was falling in love.

Well, my mother noticed that far-away look in my eyes and
told me not to forget La Mona had spent some time as a bar girl.
I told her that work was work, and I wasn't interested in her past.
Then one day we were in a canoe together going along the shore,
and I told her how I felt. My words surprised her, and her face
flushed. I took that as a "yes" and that was that. I went to her
father and, before he could say anything at all, told him how I
felt. The old man nodded and said, "Look, boy, you're the son
of a hard-working man, and, because of that, you deserve her.
But show me you can support her by building a farm here on
my land."

I went to it and, a year later had a lot cleared, a house built,
and a vegetable garden planted.

"Go and have a look," I told him.

"Now go and talk to her," was his answer.

I didn't have to. She already knew, as a woman who is born
for a man knows, and we were married by the law and the
church in Pinillos. It was during the marriage preparation course
that I met Father Javier. I never had much use for priests, but
Father Javier was a fine man. Instead of preaching at you, he just
talked to you and, you could feel a genuine friendship there. We
became friends, and La Mona and I liked to take time off work

when we could to talk to him.

My father fell ill. He'd been struck on the head with a piece of wood when he was younger, and now, as an old man, he had a discharge coming from one of his ears and had a hard time breathing. My brother's death drained the life right out of him. I was busy working the land my father-in-law had given us and doing what I could to keep my father's farm going because my brothers had all left. The older ones left to start their own lives, and the younger ones left to move in with my mother. My parents had gone their separate ways for reasons of their own, and my mother lived in a little place we'd made for her in Pinillos.

My mother and father hated each other so much it scared us, to the point that sometimes it seemed they wanted to kill each other, after living together, suffering together, and bringing up all of us kids. People who love each other a lot when they're young can end up hating each other when they're old. That's the way things are, and, when that happens to your parents, it's best to leave them alone and not take sides.

I also cut wood and sold it to Puertas de Colombia, a company that bought anything and everything you could sell it and never shied away from doing business with anyone. Marijuana was still around, as were the corruption, the killings, and the women that went with it. All of those little villages—Tiquisio, La Raya, Tacuyalta, El Colorado, and El Sudán—became little more than bars with a street running through them, and the teenaged girls—even the little girls—turned into bar girls. You'd find bodies regularly in the ditches. The businessmen and authorities in the towns were all making money off marijuana one way or another, and the killings became an everyday thing. Everyone knew what was going on, but, if you wanted to stay alive, you didn't say anything to anybody. We'd talk about it to Father Javier because we trusted one another, but that was as far as it went.

It was in those days that we started to hear people talk about "los muchachos"—that they were so and so; that they'd come from such and such a place and were headed someplace else. Nothing specific. Until one day, I was opening up a channel on the river to tow some wood through, and I ran right into them. There were eight or ten of them—I was so scared I didn't even count them—armed and wearing uniforms. They asked to see my *cédula,* asked about what I did and who I knew, made some notes, and left. I didn't hear anything more about them for weeks. Then, around the beginning of 1995, they sent word to all the farmers that they wanted to see them in Achí. We went to the meeting, and they were direct in what they said.

"We are going to stay around here. We won't tolerate drugs. We won't tolerate informants. We won't tolerate criminals. If you are one, you'd better leave. If you aren't, do your work, keep to yourself, and don't bother anyone else. Anyone who breaks our law will get two chances before we kill him or her. The first, to correct their mistake. The second, to go. The third is the end."

That's all they said. People back through the rivers and mountains in this region had seen them around for years. I think they came out to talk in town, though, because it's in the towns where the people and the money are. They struck me as being too bitter. I saw them again when they got people together to build a bridge, and we'd hear about them from time to time, but they were always like smoke in the wind.

Our talks with Father Javier led to meetings with the community and work projects for the benefit of the community. We organized groups, workshops, and bazaars with people in the countryside, and I began to enjoy the work. I think La Mona enjoyed it even more than I did. She became a health promoter and, through her work, got to know all the region's rivers, trails, and families like the back of her hand. I'd go with her when I had the time because it pleased me to see how dedicated she was to her people and how fond they were becoming of us.

We really didn't know where it was all leading or where we would end up. You know it's strange, but sometimes you get an inkling of what's going to happen before it happens. I'm not sure why, but it's as if you get a warning of something bad on the way. Sometimes I think you bring it on yourself by dwelling on thoughts that are just passing through your mind quickly.

Well, one day both of my chainsaws broke. A little while later, we had to take my father to the hospital and leave him in Pinillos. On the way back, we capsized and almost drowned in Brazo de Loba, and then, when I got home, I found La Mona in terrible shape after spilling some boiling water on her leg. One of my brothers had shown up from Cartagena, where he worked unloading ships in the port. He seemed nervous, wound up, and restless to me, but I didn't dwell on it. The trip, I thought to myself. But La Mona said, "No, it's not the trip. He's running away from something."

The days passed, and we all forgot about that until he went into town on July 20 with my little brother who was twelve. They walked around until they ran into a couple of friends. We found out later they were former EPL guerrillas who had demobilized. Well, they drank a couple of *biches* together and, just as they were leaving to come home, the *paracos* got them. They killed both my brothers. The others shot their way out of there.

They told us what happened, and I went into town feeling

like a dead man on my way out of this world. I walked into the police station like a zombie. No one knew what had happened, they said, and no one had seen anything. The police looked at us like you look at a dead animal. Father Javier was there as well, trying to console my parents who couldn't stop crying.

We had the wake in the priest's house, and, while we were sitting there, the killers came back. They were so sure of themselves there in town they didn't even have their faces covered. I couldn't accept them killing my little brother like that. Lorenzo was his name. He was just an innocent creature who hadn't done any harm to anybody. His only crime was growing up and tagging along with his brother. Looking at his face there in the casket, I couldn't control my tears. How could anyone murder such a little angel? And then, as if shedding his blood wasn't enough, shoot the coffin full of holes? Bastards!

Wicked men. Only men born of Satan himself could do such a thing. I cried for my older brother as well, because there is nothing in the world as valuable as a human life. It's worth more than a piece of land, more than an idea, or a even a fortune in money. But he died as he lived, even though we found out it was to get back at the former guerrillas that they'd shot him. All the same, he'd at least lived a little and knew something of what life was all about. But the little one, for God's sake. "Why? Why, God? Where's your justice, where's your sword?" I prayed.

Without us having anything to do with it, the guerrillas attacked the town several days later and destroyed the police station, leaving nothing but rubble where it had stood.

"Let's go talk to them on the other side," I said to La Mona.

Father Javier was in the same boat with us that day. The police in Pinillos were building a new police station in the middle of the park and making everyone help.

"Anyone who doesn't help is a delinquent, and that's how we'll treat him," said the navy captain who arrived to supervise the work. The new police station looked like a copy of the colonial fortress walls in Cartagena, and we decided to go to Medellín and stay with La Mona's aunt and uncle until the fear left us. It's a dangerous emotion, fear, very treacherous. Father Javier was from Medellín, and he put in a good word for me to the priest in the Buenos Aires barrio where I started to work teaching the catechism. It didn't take me long to see how much suffering there was around there and how it was the same suffering as my own. La Monita, God bless her, never let me sink too deep in that sea of sorrow.

When you are really suffering, you look for others who are suffering to share and help carry the burden. So I was grateful when they put me in charge of catechizing the barrio's orphans. The wars between drug cartels in the city had left many kids in the streets without parents or brothers and sisters or anyone else to look out for them. I heard many sad stories from them, children who had seen their parents and their whole families murdered. They all harbored that pain in their souls, pain so terrible that none spoke of it. As time passed, though, I began to feel homesick and to miss all the people I cared for.

I longed for the rivers, the noise of the motorboat on the river, and the humid, sticky heat and storms that shook the sky. I couldn't get used to waking up and working every day inside four plastic walls. I missed my friends, talking to my brothers over a cup of coffee, arguing with my neighbors, the mayor's lies, the Indians' complaints, even the times when we were hungry and afraid. In spite of my work and the peace of mind it gave me, I didn't feel any life under my feet. When it all became too much for me, I told La Mona I was leaving.

"All right," she said. "But you are not going to leave us alone, are you?"

"Leave who alone?" I answered, without understanding what she meant by "us."

"The baby and me," she said, her voice full of emotion.

"What?"

"Yes, I'm pregnant."

The news made me happy. When I'd recovered from the surprise, I said to her, "Mona, now we have even more reason to go back. I don't want our baby to be born into this slum."

"Let's go," she agreed. "God will guide us."

Going home means remembering your past and where you come from. The river seemed smaller than I remembered, the people tougher, and life less agreeable. But it was our river, they were our people, and it was our life. I had sworn on the body of my little brother and in the lonely times in Medellín that I'd spend the rest of my life working for the good of the community.

So as soon as I stepped ashore in Pinillos, I went to the Organización Campesina del Bajo Cauca, an organization the church helped set up to defend our rights and to improve our living conditions. The main problem was still the ranchers and lumber men and their greed for land. They were paying next to nothing for all the wood and land they could get their hands on. Abuses were commonplace, and day laborers were forced to work for a miserable wage or lose their jobs. It was all as clear as the nose on your face. The bishop of Barranca understood it, and we campesinos understood it, too.

Time passed. The guerrillas grew stronger, and the lumber men and large landowners closed ranks against them. Somehow we managed to continue on with our work. Then the government began talking about building a road to Tiquisio, and it sparked a land war, as everyone scrambled for land close to the future road site knowing it would skyrocket in value. The lumber merchants hurried to cut and sell as much wood as they could, and the ranchers and speculators rushed to grab as much land as possible to sell back to the government when it started the road.

There were more robberies, more abuses, and more killings, and, as a result, all the organizations working to defend campesino rights united against this mad rush to push people from the land and the violence that was being used to do it. When the church in its way and the guerrillas in their way threw in with the people, the paramilitaries and the army appeared. And impunity, which cements their marriage, put down roots and came to stay as well.

The laws in defense of our rights were clear. But consciousness-raising work with people to decide who the usurpers were and who we should fight against was time-consuming and very difficult. God's word isn't written in our everyday language, and it was almost impossible to understand how following the laws could be more Christian than following the scriptures, which was what we were doing, or at least trying to do.

Loving your neighbor means fighting at his side. But figuring out where that side is, is a test God gives us. That's when faith saves us and when it moves mountains, because only faith can show us what has to be done and where it is. In Pinillos, we worked with a group from the church helping to organize communities, holding workshops, setting up community work groups, doing communal projects, and helping with any other groups people wanted to get involved in. All this, because if people have come to understand anything at all, it is that, alone, we can do nothing, are nothing, and don't exist.

The Organización Campesina del Bajo Cauca expanded its work throughout the region, from Magangué to Nechí and from Ayapel to El Banco. I had, and have, a map of the whole region in my head because I'd walked it, traveled its rivers, and suffered with its people. In fact, I was coming back from a meeting in Calzón Blanco the day the paracos attacked Pinillos and killed those fourteen people. Most of them had been working with the church or were simply Christians Levis had no use for.

La Mona went back to Medellín, to those cold and far-off mountains, with our son Lorenzo. She'd rather sell *chontaduro* in the Parque Berrío, because the noise of the city streets distracts her from thoughts of the last massacre and the silence it left in her soul. She had a lost and weary expression on her face when she left, like the water that carries the bodies along in the Cauca river.

As for me, I'm still with my people. We've stopped running and decided to resist. Without weapons or a thirst for vengeance, but with the land we've worked and made something of together. The land that is us all. We live at night. During the day, we stick to the jungle, where we've built our shelters and set up a village under the trees. We eat from a communal pot. Each person puts in what they can and takes what they need to keep on living and resisting this plague of blood that God has put in our path. They can hurt us and do to us as they will, but we won't give in.

Chapter 5

The Turkish Boat

I

Toñito was the last child Father Eustaquio baptized during his evangelizing crusade. The proof of that is that all his younger friends have non-Christian names: Bryan, Wilmer, Hayler. Franciscan priests used to come by each year to baptize the children who had been born and marry their parents. But they hadn't been back since the paisas *began to overrun the land along the Atrato River, setting up sawmills to exploit the tropical wood and then becoming involved*

The passages in italics are those of a doctor/counselor in a Cartagena hospital who decides to adopt the child narrator of the chapter, Toñito.

in drug trafficking. Life would never again be as it was when the women would ask San Lorenzo in song to favor them with a breeze to blow away the husks of the rice they were stripping.

Toño grew up on the shores of the Chajeradó River. He learned to swim before he learned to walk and spent much of his boyhood watching the women squatting on wooden planks washing clothes in the river. Wooden planks are used because there are no stones in that land. A stone there is a treasure. Toño didn't go to school because there wasn't one to go to and because no one was interested in learning to read when there were radios around. The adults could add and subtract just enough to figure out what they were owed by the sawmills in Riosucio—three days downriver—where they sold their wood. Neither Toñito nor anyone else knows how or why they arrived to burn down their houses, and he still trembles with fear when he talks about what he has been through since that morning.

I was making a wooden top because I was bored playing with boats and kites. The rice wasn't ready to be harvested yet, and we still had some time to play, because when it's ready, it's like when the river overflows—there's no place you can hide to rest. The men cut it with machetes, and the women carried it to the village. The children had to run errands, and the adults would never leave us alone. We'd take *biche* to the men, so they wouldn't be bored, and water with lemon to the women, so they could stand the sun. The bad thing about being a kid is that we have to do all the things no one else likes to do and keep going when everybody else is resting.

Making tops is difficult. There's nothing to round them off with, so they'll keep spinning and not fall over. The best ones are

made out of *chachajo*. It's a hard wood to work with, and that's
why they last. What I liked best was making boats and letting
them float off downriver as far away as they could go. I liked to
watch them from the shore until I couldn't see them anymore.
The boats going upriver and the logs floating down drowned a
lot of my boats, but I kept on making them because I wanted
one of them to make it all the way to the ocean. My father used
to say that all water flows to the ocean. And my grandfather
thought he'd go there to die. It's true. The river carries everything
to the ocean: the branches and fronds lightning knocks down;
the rice that falls down the riverbank into the water; the clothes
and running shoes you leave by the water to dry; animals that
are too sure of themselves and their strength; and even the
garbage you throw away.

I used balsa to carve all the big boats I saw on the Atrato
when I'd go to Riosucio with my uncle Anselmo to sell *cativo*
logs. In Riosucio, the boats are as big as houses. They have ceil-
ings, stoves, and televisions inside them, and, on some of them,
chickens are even raised. You could live your whole life on a boat
like that without ever getting off. Why would you want to get
off if you have everything you need right there with you? The
big boats go as far as Cartagena, towing logs there and bringing
back consignments and dishes. It takes two days to go and two
days to come back. My uncle told me there were even bigger
boats in the ocean, but I didn't believe him. I didn't believe him
even though he was my friend and taught me about the jungle
and some of its ways, like how a bite from a *mapaná* snake can
kill a steer before you can even find out where it was bitten, or
how a jaguar can punch a hole in the side of a boat with its paw,
or how a thorn from the *chonta* palm can puncture a rubber

boot and pass right through it.

My uncle Anselmo had seen a lot of places. He'd been to Quibdó and to Istmina, where the water flows backwards and goes into the other ocean, and he'd worked in the sawmill at the mouth of the León River where people bring logs from all the rivers. One day, he got into an argument with the bosses about some money they owed but didn't want to pay him. He ended up hitting one of them a couple of times with the flat part of his machete, leaving him gasping for air like a fish out of water. The police went after my uncle for that, and, once he got home, he didn't go back.

He started thinking about the whole lumber business, though, and began doing the arithmetic in his head: here they pay us so much, in Riosucio so much, and by the León River so much. I wonder what the wood would be worth in Cartagena? Well, when he got brave after figuring all that out and told the sawmill workers along the Curvaradó River about it, they killed him—beat him unconscious and drowned him. He floated by the mouth of the Murrí three days later swollen up like a manatee and as white as a bleached *paisa*. My grandfather said it was a death better left alone and that vengeance would only bring more killing. But no one listened to him, and there were killings here and there until the lumber business came to an end.

One day the guerrillas came by, men who carried guns and knew the jungle. No one had seen them before. They were on their way somewhere else and had two wounded men with them, all skin and bones like the Holy Christ at Buchadó. They asked for help. Everyone was curious about people who showed up in the village, and they always helped them. The guerrillas rested, slept, ate, and washed their clothes. They were nervous about the wounded men who looked paler and paler each night. Nothing we tried—not medicinal waters, herbs, or prayers—did them any good. They died because they'd lost too much blood, and we buried them in the cemetery, hidden a little bit. The commander told us we couldn't say anything about them to anybody.

"If you do," he said, "we'll be back, and it won't be to ask what happened."

But the days passed and times got worse. People along the Curvaradó River lived on rice and plantain soup for three years because they refused to give their wood away at unfair low prices—until more paisas arrived with their packs full of business offers they said couldn't fail. Many were interested right away and started in with the coca: planting, picking, and working it and filling their bags with money. At first, no one showed any losses or ran any risks, and the outsiders paid on time as they said they would. I saw what was going on because I kept my eyes open and got around. I dreamed of leaving. Getting away from the river, going to Cartagena, and seeing the ocean.

The coca business has a force to it like water when you try to hold it back, and people who get into it can't get out. My mother had no use for people who lived chasing after money, but other people saw coca as a way out and threw themselves into it body and soul. Then, one day, the coca buyers showed up armed and angry.

"From now on, we're paying so much and no more. Like it or not. We know you are helping the guerrillas, and we won't put up with it anymore."

"That wasn't the agreement," my grandfather told them. "And if you're not going to pay what you said you were, then we won't do any more business with you."

The men in the village nodded their agreement.

"Guerrilla sons-of-bitches! That's why you don't want to work with us," said the devils.

The men said no more, and there was nothing left to do. The coca changed hands at the new price they set, and they left without another word. We all thought that was the end of it, that it wouldn't go any further than threats, but my grandfather knew better: "No. They'll be back. We'd better leave here and hide in the hills."

And they came back. My grandfather woke up many times in the night. I thought it was to pee because I used to see him other nights getting up swaying a little from side to side. Then he'd go outside and come back looking relieved. But this time it was something else. The animals were uneasy too that night, and I told myself that if the dogs weren't barking, no one was coming. I remember it was just as light was beginning to appear that we heard the first shouts.

"Guerrilla sons-of-bitches! We're going to burn down your houses! Come out so we can see your faces!"

"Get in behind the sacks of rice and don't make a sound. You'll be all right there," my grandfather told me as he left the house.

They killed him right there in the doorway. He fell beside me, but I couldn't even reach out my hand to him to feel the last of his warmth.

They began dragging the adults out and tying them together like pieces of wood they were going to throw into the river. The women were screaming and crying, and the children were running all around. The devil commander was shooting as if we were *guatines*.

I was petrified and couldn't move. When I managed to suck in some air to breathe, the breaths made a noise that made me shake with fear. People were running everywhere, and, in the village, there was only pain. Then, as if prompted by my grandfather, I took off running out the door and toward the hills. No one else was running in that direction and the shots followed me. The devils were shooting everywhere. I passed bodies lying in the yards; bodies between the houses and by the wharf. Anyone the devils grabbed, they killed with their machetes. I don't know how I ran so much. I'd fall down and bounce up again as if I'd fallen on springs and keep on running. I'd cut myself on the branches and the thorns, and it only felt like something tickling me.

I ran until I couldn't hear the screams anymore, far from the river. I don't think people had ever been there because the jungle was so thick it was dark. I'd run so much that it had become night. I couldn't get away from the mosquitoes. There was a cloud of them around me, and it was like you could grab a handful of them if you tried, but I couldn't get any with my hands. Then I began to feel cold. I'd almost never felt cold, but I did now because it came along with fear. Fear that someone would find me and fear that no one would find me. Fear of the night and the jaguars. Fear of all the people they'd killed and fear that my parents and family were among them. Fear that they hadn't been killed but were wandering lost in the jungle. Fear always decides what face to show you, and it's terrible when it shows you many faces and you can't hide from any of them.

I woke up to the sun's heat. The fear had left me during the night, and, now, it was hunger that I felt. I said to myself better to die alone than have them kill me, so I won't go anywhere. I spent the day close by, searching for seeds my grandfather had shown me I could eat. When night fell, the fear returned, and a stomach ache came with it. When the mosquitoes left, I began to hear the noises of bigger animals: the owls, which didn't scare me, and the growl that monkeys make to keep jaguars away. The monkeys imitate the jaguar so well it fools even the female jaguar. I'd hear them in one place, then in another, and then they'd seem to be back where I'd first heard them. I prayed to the Cristo de los Milagros and, in his presence, fell asleep.

The next morning when I woke up I thought to myself, no, it's better to go and look for death than to wait for it to find me. But I'd walked so far, I didn't know what direction to go in. The waters will carry you along, I remembered my grandfather telling me, and I began to follow a stream. It led me to another bigger one, and, finally, I came out above the river. By walking along the shore, I came to the village, abandoned, empty, and silent. Not even the sound of the wind. There was no one there who could tell me if anyone was still alive.

Someone had dug up some of the bodies, and the dogs were scattering their remains all over the place. I sat down where they killed my grandfather and started crying. I couldn't find his body or the bodies of any of my family, only a trail of blood leading down to the river.

I cried and cried there, finally going down to the river to wait for someone to come along and take me away downriver. But in spite of my cries and my waving, none of the boats that passed by came near me. No one wanted to have anything to do with what had happened in the village so as not to have to tell the authorities anything. Everybody knew, but nobody wanted to know.

I walked along the shore downriver until I lost sight of the village. A boat picked me up in the afternoon. Everyone on it was talking about what had happened in my village and what they'd done to us. They said the bodies had been thrown in the river, so they wouldn't be recognized and that some had been cut open so they wouldn't float. The ones that had been thrown in "whole," they said, would show up in three days down by the mouth of the Moya de los Chulos. They said vultures sat on the bodies as they floated along. They were swollen up like bladders, and the birds picked at them with their beaks until they'd burst and sink down out of sight.

When I heard that, I started to pray my parents hadn't been cut open or picked open by the vultures and that I'd be able to at least pray over their bodies. When we got to la Moya, I told the man I wanted to get off. I wasn't alone there, and there were others from my village waiting for the third day to see who would float by. The women were praying at an altar they'd set up to the Señor Milagroso, and the men were drinking biche and talking quietly. Everyone was waiting to pick up their loved ones and bury them. One of my neighbors named Doña Edelmira swore that bodies that sink in the river turn into fish.

Late in the afternoon, the first body came by, and they pulled it out. It was Don Anastasio, the owner of a store called *Mi Orgullo* [My Pride]. He looked bloated and didn't have any eyes. They pulled him out of the water in pieces, prayed for him, and put him in a hole. There was no one from his family there. A while later, a cousin of mine floated in.

"That one's mine," I shouted. They hauled him up on shore and helped me bury him. I felt important because everyone paid me their respects, but was sad because he was family.

By early the next morning, the river was full, so many that there weren't enough holes to put them all in. All you could hear was: "that one's mine," "that one's mine." I felt cold seeing so many bodies. But my family, the ones I was waiting for, weren't among them. As each body came by, I thought it would be my father, my mother, or one of my brothers or sisters. But no. As much as I'd look and look at them as they floated in and expect it, none of my loved ones were among them. You need to see the body of a person who dies, so you can cry for him and put the rage that death makes you feel inside to rest. Without a body, the dead person stays alive, hovering around the living like horseflies around cattle.

The devils arrived that afternoon and told everyone to leave the bodies alone. They said if anybody tried to fish one out, it would have company on its way downriver. We got on a boat and left there with the last family to go, the Mosqueras. There was nothing else to do. After a while, we came up alongside Vigia del Fuerte, and we could see the mayor's office, the police station, and the bank were all in ruins and smoking.

"It was the guerrillas paying them back for what happened in Chajeradó," someone said. No one else said anything.

My grandfather was right, I thought to myself.

The boat continued down the river slowly; the motor hypnotizing me with its steady cadence. Half asleep, I awoke suddenly when my head banged into the side of the boat. A wave had almost capsized the boat. I rubbed my eyes a couple of times but couldn't figure out where we were. The river had opened up into a huge swamp.

"The gulf's choppy today," said one of the sailors, and, just then, we turned a corner, and I saw the ocean before me. I began to shake just looking at it and smelling that smell that comes up from its depths. I was overcome with emotion and remember opening my arms wide like a bird stretching its wings and beginning to cry like a newborn baby. It was as if all that immensity was washing over me and my pain. By the time we stepped ashore in Turbo, I had arranged with the captain to continue on to Cartagena in exchange for washing the boat and helping tie it up when we docked.

II

Toñito was brought to the hospital in critical condition. I was just finishing my shift in emergency, and they brought him in comatose. He was suffering from what I thought was going to be a fatal hypothermia as a result of being in the water so long. We worked on him and were gradually able to bring him back to life.

It's a short story. Toñito had stowed away on a Turkish ship that sailed for New York. He was discovered by some sailors during the trip, and the captain ordered them to throw him overboard. Toñito didn't fight or struggle but, instead, jumped into the ocean by himself. He'd never been afraid of water. He'd been born by water and had been around it all his life. A ship's deck can be twenty-five meters high, though, and, when he hit the water it stunned him. But it didn't kill him. The turbulence from the propellers almost drowned him, but Toñito knew not to fight the current and, instead, let himself be carried by it. He watched as the boat sailed away and the calm returned.

He floated for a long time. He knew he could never swim to shore, and that knowledge saved him from desperation. He floated for more than three hours until some fishermen on their way back from the islands of Barú rescued him. When they picked him up, they thought he was dead. They rubbed him with turtle oil to warm him up and gave him coconut water until he started to breathe. Just breathing, though, isn't the same as coming to your senses, and that's why they brought him here to the hospital. I'd sit with him when he started to eat, and he'd look at me with a grateful expression on his face. He said he'd decided to leave Cartagena and go "wherever the wind took him" because in Cartagena they'd tried to "set him on fire."

I lived with a gang in the street. We hustled anywhere we could. There were four of us: three from the Chocó and one from a town called Chengue in the Montes de María. We ate whatever we could find during the day, and, at night, we slept on the street outside some of the fancy stores by the automatic bank machines or under cars. Everywhere we went people would beat on us saying we were thieves, that we were dirty and smelly. We were always running from the police, and, when the guards and watchmen got their hands on us, they'd kick us around. We thought selling coconut oil on the beach was a good business, but we couldn't get started because the ones there made a deal with the police—paid them—so they could have all the business for themselves. We couldn't go near the hotels because they had guards who used billy clubs during the day and machetes during the night. Sometimes the tourists wanted to give us some money, but the police wouldn't let them. They said we used *basuco* and sold coke. Coke? We didn't even have enough money to buy food! Sometimes we'd sniff glue, especially when we were hungry or cold, because it's like a blanket that warms you up and fills your gut. The police and the watchmen are the ones who sell the coke and marijuana.

The gang came out of the Mandela barrio. That's where
everybody who has nowhere to live ends up. As soon as I stepped
ashore in the port of Cartagena, I headed for Mandela. One of
the sailors told me: "Go there. You'll make out all right, and you
might even run into your father and mother."

Just the thought of seeing them again, even for a short time,
cheered me up. That's what you hope when someone goes away,
that you'll see them again and be able to tell them you're still
alive. The thought that my family had been killed thinking that I
was already dead tormented me because it would have made them
even sadder. But then, sometimes, I think the devils probably
didn't give them enough time to think about anything at all.

There are thousands of families in Mandela, and all of them
arrived fleeing from something, leaving a trail of death behind.
They want to go on living, and they have to accept life as it comes.
You don't bargain with destiny once you've looked death in the
face. There were a lot of people from communities along the
Atrato and some from the Chajeradó in Mandela. Cartagena has
always been kind of like the mother of all those rivers, the place
you head for if things are going badly or if they're going well. The
first thing I thought when I got to Mandela was that the devils
who'd destroyed my village were probably there. But then I
thought they couldn't possibly kill us with so many people around.

The first night I walked into the barrio, I ran into Don Tato,
one of my father's cousins. He was a good man, and I felt happy
thinking he would ask me to stay with him as was the custom
along the rivers. Anyone who arrives there, even on a stormy
night, has somewhere to stay and something to eat, no questions
asked. But, before I had even opened my mouth, he told me,
"Life here isn't like what you're used to. Here, it's every man for

himself. None of that, 'Remember that favor I did for you such and such a time? I was just wondering if I could…' Here, there's none of that! You don't use your hands to get by here, you use your elbows, to push people out of the way! Believe me, it's not that I don't want to help. It's that I can't. It's either you survive or I survive. So we'll see you later."

I was stunned and thought, well, maybe he's just in a bad mood, but surely everyone doesn't think like that. But no one wanted to let me stay in their shack. The truth is they weren't even shacks, just boxes made of plastic and cardboard perched on the mud there by the swamp.

You had to carry the water you needed over from a pipe that turned off and on every now and again and the bathroom was a ditch that everybody used, but no one ever covered up. I wandered around until I saw a woman who didn't look like she was from there. There was a child beside her crying and screaming, and I said that if she wanted me to, I could pick her up and rock her a little. She said no, that the child was crying because she was hungry and holding her wasn't going to change that. I told her, "If you let me stay in a corner of your place, I'll help you with it and look for food for both of us."

"Have a look and see, then," she answered.

I moved in with them. I hardly ever slept because the little girl cried day and night, and all the woman gave her was rice water. I'd go out early and bring something back for them in the afternoon. It was during those times that I met the gang, and we started hanging around together. Some would stay put while the others hustled, and we'd get enough for us and for me to take something back. It wasn't enough though, and one morning the little girl died. She was always hungry, and I guess it just got the best of her. With her child gone, the woman sold her shack, and the new owner told me I wasn't welcome.

That turned out to be lucky for me because a couple of days after I moved out and began living in the street, the devils arrived and killed seven kids, all of them displaced from the rivers like me. I never went back to Mandela after that.

We had an agreement in the gang that anything anyone found was for all of us. No one went off looking for himself. When you're looking through garbage cans or you're hustling a tourist or breaking a window to grab something, it's easier to do if you're together. And in order to avoid arguing afterwards about who gets what, it's best to divide everything up equally.

We found enough to live and we did all right. You can start to live again when you're not always worrying about the devils. But there are many devils, the real ones and others who help them. We began squatting by the door of a store, leaving early and coming back late—until the owner got fed up and called the police. We left, but not before puncturing the tires on his car to get back at him. After that, we moved into the sewer. It was like a big hole with only one way into it.

One night at about two, I heard a sound like someone talking. The others were all high because they'd been sniffing, but I'd had a headache all day and didn't stay with them. Well, before I knew what was going on, there were flames everywhere. I yelled to the others and stumbled toward the way out. I was the first one up, and the flames were just catching, but one of my feet caught fire anyway. I got out, but the others were burned up like chickens on a spit. I found out that setting the fire had been the store owner's idea because, before dawn the next morning, without anyone having reported it, the police came by and took the bodies away in black plastic bags. But no one knew there were bodies in there except for me and the ones who set the fire. I made up my mind there and then: "I'm going. I'm going. I'm going wherever the big ships take me."

So off Toñito went on the Turkish ship. I want to adopt the boy. I've done all the paperwork, but now, the Family Welfare Institute says he isn't an orphan because his parents were never legally declared dead or disappeared and because nobody reported their disappearance. So we have to wait and see if anyone comes forward to claim him, or his parents show up and go to the Institute looking for him. This will all mean several years of waiting and more paperwork. Judging by how long it takes for the paperwork to be done, Toñito will turn eighteen before the judge renders a decision and I can adopt him.

Chapter 6

The Garden

When you're young, you think life is a bed of roses, but as you grow older, you realize they're all full of thorns.

I'll never forget the day they killed Don Raúl. I had my first communion that morning, and even though my white dress with orange blossoms on it was rented, I didn't want to take it off. I felt pure in that dress, like one of the pure souls Father Aniceto had told us about during the forty days of Lent, which was the preparation period for me to receive the body of Jesus.

My father adored me, and he'd brought some musicians from Chaparral to play at the party. It was wonderful. Right in the middle of it, some men burst in and shot Don Raúl. He was giving me a present, a book called *The Imitation of Christ,* by Thomas Kempis, which I never read more than the title of because the letters were too small.

Don Raúl tried to tell them not to kill him, but they'd already done it. The shot him in the face, and the blood splattered on me like a frightened animal, staining the dress I'd received the baby Jesus in. The blood was hot and smelled like copper, and, to this day, I haven't been able to forget that smell. His eyes were skewed in opposite directions as if he'd been trying to pick out his killers but couldn't find them among all the people. Five women and the children he'd given each of them wept for Don Raúl at the funeral. Wailed as though they were fighting over the body and revealing secrets, each knowing he hadn't been much of a husband. We never knew for sure who killed him, but he wasn't a man of the law, so they probably did it as a warning to others.

I'm still paying the price for having been splattered with that blood and seeing those eyes, and, even now, at thirty-seven years old, I can't sleep in a dark room without seeing Don Raúl standing at the foot of the bed or lying on the floor with his tongue hanging out of his mouth, like he ended up. It's as if I still owe him something.

In spite of that nightmare, though, I had a happy childhood, mostly because I was the apple of my father's eye. He used to talk to me with his eyes, and I always understood what he didn't put into words. We were very close. He was a good man, kind to us at home and to the neighbors, in spite of the fact *La Violencia* had hurt him deeply. He told me he hoped we'd never be harmed in any way, and, when he prayed on Sundays, he asked God to keep us safe from the war, so we wouldn't have to go through what he did.

He used to tell us stories of those days and how he had to hide in the hills from the *chulavitas*, so they wouldn't kill him. And how he'd gone from hiding like an animal to joining the guerrillas and the places they'd gone: all through the Cañón de las Hermosas, up the Amoyá River to the top of the mountain, over the other side to the Atá River, and down the Amoyá as far as Saldaña. They turned over their weapons to the army during the Rojas government—getting nothing in return that time—and that's when he met my mother.

He was still with the guerrillas the first time he saw her. My mother says he'd stop to talk sometimes when they were going by or ask after her and leave if she wasn't around. He wouldn't be wearing a uniform or carrying a gun when they talked, and, when he left, she thought it would be the last time she'd see him. But he came back after they'd turned over their weapons and said he would no longer be a guerrilla. Flirting with her, he said she was to blame, that it was because of her eyes the guerrillas stopped fighting.

One time, my father introduced me to a friend of his from the old days. He was very much like my father. They started reminiscing and talking about how everybody that lived in the area back then had led the same kind of life—gone off the same way and married the girls they met on their travels. They'd buried their pasts, their battles, and the war, and dedicated themselves to being who they were—country people.

They were like one, big family living on the land together, Indian land because my father and his parents and almost everyone else in those hills are half Indian and have rights to the land Quintín Lame* fought for and won in Yaguará and Calarma. My father even had claim to part of the Yarí reservation, which was land the government turned over to the campesinos on the plains of Caquetá to build a town, land they cleared and worked in spite of the fact that when the air force plane dumped them there with their families, dogs, and chickens that Sunday in 1961, they didn't even know how to start a fire. There were no fish left in the rivers of the Yaguará and no animals in the *cordillera*, and it was the Indians there who taught them how to fish and hunt again. And showed them how they could eat flour instead of rice and drink *chicha* made from *pipire*—or *chontaduro,* as we call it here—instead of beer.

I never went to Yarí, thank God, because my family—my aunts, uncles, and cousins—were bombed there by the same air force in 1997. The military was looking for Marulanda** and carried out the bombing as a retaliation for having to demilitarize Cartagena del Chairá to get back the soldiers the guerrillas captured after Las Delicias. We found out soldiers used to shoot at the women and children washing their clothes in the Tunia River—for fun, just to see them run away.

I was bored at home in Tolima. My brothers were always complaining to my father that I should be doing more work and reading fewer books. Learning from books was important to me. I wanted to improve myself, and all their complaining just showed me how dumb they were. My father decided to send me

---

* Leader of indigenous uprisings that sought to expel white settlers from indigenous lands in the Cauca region in the 1910s.

** Manuel Marulanda Velez, alias of Pedro Antonio Marín, legendary FARC guerrilla founder and leader.

away from Ortega to live with an aunt in Armenia. I know it was hard for him to do because when we said goodbye he didn't want to look me in the eye, and, when he finally did, his eyes were sad and lifeless.

I was very unhappy in Armenia. My aunt was a prude and made me say the rosary and go to Mass on Sundays and holidays. The school I went to was run by nuns, and they were envious and bitter. They had so much sin hidden away and spent all day talking about virtue. One of them fell in love with me, and she'd look at me day and night with a glazed expression on her face. Her hands were always sweaty, and she repulsed me because she smelled like false teeth. I loathed her, and, what's worse, she taught gym and was in charge of the nurse's office and the school office, so, even if you didn't want to see her, you were always running into her.

I always had a headache at school and got my period early, and, ever since then, my head always hurts when I have it. I never said anything about it to her—Sister Encarnación was her name—or went to the nurse's office, because every chance she'd get she'd make you lie down on a little stretcher and start feeling your "glands." Who knew where she thought they were. Anyway, I quit school after grade five and left my aunt's house and went to work in a stationery store.

When I turned eighteen in Armenia, my father came to get me. He still had the same sad-looking eyes, and he didn't like the fact that I was working in a store, serving customers. His favorite daughter had no business serving anyone or living in a dirty, run-down rented room. He asked me to come back home with him, so I could go back to school or learn a craft or trade.

My brothers weren't there when I got back to the farm in

San José de las Hermosas. They'd moved on to jobs elsewhere. Soon after arriving home, I began to hear about someone named Alvaro. Everyone talked about him: Alvaro brought the groceries; Alvaro took care of the horses; Alvaro milked the cows and took the milk to Chaparral. Alvaro this and Alvaro that.

After a month back home, I still hadn't seen hide nor hair of this Alvaro. My father enrolled me in a dressmaking class in Chaparral, so I wouldn't waste my time waiting for school to start and, one day, as we were walking across the plaza in town, someone called out to me. I didn't answer—spoiled and full of myself as I was—or even stop to acknowledge him and walked away. Then my sister stopped me, saying,

"Look, it's Alvaro."

"That's the Alvaro everybody talks so much about?" I said. "I expected something a little different."

He asked if he could walk with me, and I said no thank you. Later, as I was buying something in a store, there he was again. I told him I didn't think my father would like him bothering me, but he said not to worry about that. Well, he hardly ever left me alone after that. When I'd get out of class, he'd be waiting for me. I told my sisters I thought he was a real bore. Gradually, though, his persistence paid off and he started to win me over. That's why it's better not to talk too much about something you don't want. You might have to eat your words later.

I remember one time the lights had gone out and it was dark when I left class, and I was a little nervous. Since Alvaro lived in front of our house, I agreed to let him walk me home. We started talking after that and began to see each other almost every day. I realized he wasn't as boring as I'd thought.

When they started kidding me at home and asked me if we

were a "couple," I said it was just something to pass the time for a little while. Well, that little while stretched out into seventeen years and six children. We didn't get married; we just went off together. My mother nagged me constantly at home, and I was bored. And since I knew what it was like to live alone, away from my family, I decided to go with Alvaro.

When I told my mother I was going, she grabbed one of my father's belts and hit me twice on the legs as if I were an eight-year-old again. It left two burn-like marks on my skin, and I ran out of the house furious. I took a suitcase with me, thinking I'd go into town and wait there until she went looking for me and said she was sorry. But I ran into Alvaro, and we decided there and then to leave for good.

We went to Ibagué and talked to a priest about wanting to live together. He said we had to get married and that he'd have to talk to my parents first. Well, I told him that was impossible because my father had thrown me out of the house. It was a lie. My father had never done that, never even touched me. I just wanted to get back at my mother. Marriage or priests didn't mean anything to me then, and they still don't. The priest treated us like sinners, saying only God knew where we'd end up if we didn't get married in church and have children according to His law. Faced with all that silliness, we decided to leave without getting married.

I got pregnant two weeks later. I was happy to feel that creature growing inside me, but it died three months later of broncho-pneumonia. Then I became pregnant again. Alvaro was working in construction, and we lived in a room I'd begun to paint and fix up for the baby so it'd have a special place to be loved. We had the crib in one corner with a box for diapers and clothes under it. We didn't know whether it would be a boy or a girl.

But as my time came closer, fear began gnawing at me like it had the day they'd killed Don Raúl, fear my baby would die too. I was happy and sad and afraid all at once and thought I'd go crazy. But I had a little girl and she was healthy. I couldn't rid myself of the fear, however, and I'd check her every couple of minutes to make sure the blanket in the crib hadn't smothered her. I was afraid a mouse would bite her or a fly would sting her or a draft would make her sick. I didn't let anyone see her because I didn't want anyone putting a spell on her. I believed in that.

From Ibagué we moved to Gachetá, in Cundinamarca, and, from there, back to Chaparral, always to get work. That was our life, going wherever Alvaro could get work. It's sad. He'd get a job and do nothing but work and work, and I'd be at home doing the same.

I saw my family again in Chaparral. My father came down from the farm to visit, and I saw that same sadness in his eyes as when I said goodbye to him. I think he felt betrayed by my going away and it hurt me. But what's done is done. I only hope and pray to God that he managed to forgive me before they killed him. A couple of days before that he gave Alvaro the jeep so he could use it to take passengers between the hamlets around Rioblanco. They didn't talk much because they were both jealous. My father stayed on his farm, Alvaro and I lived in Chaparral, and we didn't visit each other much. None of us wanted to visit just to gossip when there was really nothing to say.

They killed him on Corpus Christi day. I was going up to the farm to take him a couple of pounds of peanuts. He always liked them even though he didn't have any real teeth to chew them with. Alvaro was going to take me, but the jeep broke down, so I took the ten o'clock bus. Along the way, I got a terrible pain in my stomach but tried to keep it out of my mind by thinking about my father. About halfway there, we saw the six o'clock bus on its way down. It braked to a stop as it passed and the driver said,

"Did you hear they killed Don Esteban?"

The words didn't register until all the passengers turned around to look at me, and I realized the dead man was my father. With the news came a pain in my chest and a cold that made me shake uncontrollably. Some of the passengers who knew me tried to console me, but that only made me cry harder. As we continued on, I hoped there'd been some mistake but knew in my heart there hadn't.

He was already in the coffin when we got there, because they'd killed him at dawn. My mother said a friend of his, Luisito, arrived very early, and the two had gone outside together away from the house like they needed to talk about something without her hearing it. She wasn't worried, she said, because Luisito was always around the house asking for things: "Look, Don Esteban, I wonder if you could lend me some money? Could you give me something for my kids, Don Esteban? Do you think you could let me have some *panelita*, Don Esteban?" And my father would say: "Sure, my friend, don't worry. Here you are."

Those are the thorns that stick you the deepest: the man my father helped the most was the one who killed him. The man my father helped feed and whose daughters' schooling he'd paid for. He'd probably said he didn't have enough money to buy a bull he wanted, and my father'd offered to lend him the money.

Luis not only betrayed my father but was the one who took his hat and his machete back to the house and gave them to my mother.

"Someone killed him," he said, and turned to leave when my

brother told him to stop. He'd gone out with my father that dawn without Luisito seeing him and knew what had happened. When Luis saw him, an expression deader than my father came over his face and he froze. But before my brother could say another word, he turned and ran off. My mother understood at once.

"Luis killed him."

Why was my father killed? It took us a while to find out, but we finally did. Luis lied to the guerrillas about him. He told the commander that my father had been a guerrilla with Mariachi—the one who killed Charro Negro—who used to be Tirofijo's* boss and said my father had made his money off the backs of the poor and stolen all he had. They killed him because of envy, because he was always a man of principles and someone who helped the community. My relative, Escolástico Ducuara, who is still president of the Yarí *cabildo,* can attest to that.

My mother did the best she could with what was left of the farm after that, and, in Chaparral, we had to give my father's jeep to my brother. My brothers turned into bitter men after that and began ordering people around as if everything my father had left the family was theirs and theirs alone. In order to avoid problems with them, a man everyone called El Burro gave Alvaro another jeep, so he wouldn't have to give up his route between La Marina and Rioblanco. But then, one day, he ran off the road. It wasn't a bad accident, but we had to pay for everything. And we had to pawn everything we had to do that. How else could we pay for the scratches on the passengers and the merchandise that was ruined?

Without the jeep we had no way to make a living, so, one

---

* "Sure Shot," nickname for FARC founder and leader Marulanda.

Sunday, we went into Chaparral to look for work. There used to be an office there—it's not there anymore—for skilled workers looking for employers to hire them. A very elegant and friendly lady offered us work on her farm, La Marina, near Tuluá. She painted a rosy picture of life there, saying she was paid well, provided room and board and horses, that the place was safe, and the children healthy. She also said we'd have a garden where we could grow what we wanted and keep some animals.

I wasn't sure at first. I'd learned to be wary of things that sound too good to be true. I also thought I'd have a hard time getting used to the solitary and lonely life that moving there would mean. I was so used to people and noise! But I made up my mind the day they killed a neighbor—he was just a boy— on the corner outside our house as he was drinking a pop with his girlfriend. Three men showed up and shot him. They shot her, too, but, thank God, they didn't kill her. I was scared of living with death always hovering around me, afraid the kids would have to grow up seeing more bodies like that. You try not to think too much about what's going on, even if it's right in front of you, because that only brings problems. We found out the kids had been run out of Planadas by the guerrillas and told to get out of Tolima. Well, they didn't pay much attention to that or maybe they thought the guerrillas didn't come into Chaparral—who knows? All I know is if someone gives me a chance to live somewhere else, even if I haven't done anything wrong, I'd be a fool not to take them up on it. But that was life in the town—times of blood and killing that would come and go—and you could always get caught in the middle by mistake. So with that fear in mind, having practically nothing between us and in debt up to our eyeballs, we accepted the lady's offer.

We made the trip along the cordillera, up through Las
Hermosas pass. I'd only been as far up as a farm there called
La Germania. It's in the cold mountains in a spot where the
river roars by like the devil on its way down. You can hear the
rocks being swept along like glass balls, then smashing into one
another deep down in the water with a muffled sound. The
high mountains are pretty. There are trees full of fruits that look
like candelabras. There's a tree they call *sietecueros,* with violet
and purple and deep red flowers. It shimmers in the light, and
its flowers are so bright they form a kind of mirage when you
stare at them. Higher up are the huge *fraylejones,* which look
like armies in battle formation from a distance with their crests
of flowers and dry branches like lances. When you move, they
seem to walk along with you. Some of them had their bodies
burned black by flames in summer; others were so tall it
seemed they were flying; others were short and squat like
footsoldiers or peons.

And, finally, higher still, that utter silence and wide-open
empty space that made you think you'd reached the end of the
world. Silence broken only by the labored breathing of the
horses with their noble patience as they carry you on without
knowing where they are going. I liked to talk to them and give
them advice and tell them stories to make the trip less boring for
them. I wanted to pay them back for straining so much for us,
the strain you'd see in the steam coming from their noses and in
the hot sweat lifting up off their backs.

Up and up, finally, to the summit where you can almost see
the whole country. On one side, the Magdalena River, which
you don't really see but feel, because all the other waters run to
it; on another, the Cauca River, exuding its sticky, lethargic

heat; on another, the Nevado del Tolima, standing there like a sentinel; and, on the last side, the Nevado del Huila, towering as big as an altar. The pass is called Las Hermosas because of the lagoons there—which, even on cloudy days, are blue—and the streams that flow from them, cascading down one into the other. Two of them, called Las Mellizas, the Twins, lie side by side facing the town of Barragán.

Barragán is a pretty town, ringed by *curubo* trees. It was founded by settlers from Boyacá after one of those wars in the olden days. The government offered General Neira, one of the victors, all the land he and his men could see, and that must have been a great deal given that they were sharp-eyed artillery men. But land without anyone to work it is like a machete made out of wood, so the general put his soldiers to work clearing it and building him a farm. Those *Boyacos* were restless and hard-working, especially when they realized the promises that lay beneath that black, shiny, oil-smelling earth.

We went down the mountain and came to La Marina. It was a nice-looking farm and reminded me of the land around Roncesvalles. There were coffee bushes on the lower slopes and potatoes up higher—truly holy ground where you felt you'd finally turned your back on death and had only the promise of a good future ahead.

"Ninfa, this is the life you deserve," Alvaro told me.

The farm had been abandoned for a while, so we began fixing it up the way we wanted. We bought some chickens, a couple of pigs, and a cow. Alvaro went down to town two weeks later and came back with his eyes shining and his face so full of emotion I thought his heart was going to come out his mouth. He looked as if the archangel Gabriel and all his court had appeared to him. When he calmed down, he said the lady we'd met had made him a business proposition: that we start clearing part of the land to plant a garden—for which she'd provide the seed—and that we plant corn and beans up and down the sides of the other piece of land.

The idea of planting a garden there, especially one that would make money, seemed strange to me. I didn't see how that could work, and, as Alvaro explained it all, he had a kind of malicious and innocent expression on his face—like he'd been up to no good, kind of half happy and half scared. The lady said that it was a pretty flower called *amapola,* and the pod it produced was what was making people money. Then he asked me, "Don't you think it's nice we can pretty up the view by planting some flowers?"

"Don't be a fool! I wasn't born yesterday," I answered. "Say what you want to say. It's OK. I know it's against the law. But if you've made up your mind, I'll go along. What's important is that the children know nothing about it. Other than that, we'll try to make it work."

Well, once we started figuring out how much we could make, we could hardly wait to start with the garden. Greed makes you as blind as a tree trunk and as stupid as a block of cement. Alvaro went back down to close the deal and came back with the seeds. We had no idea of the problems and pain that came with them. We were selling our souls to the devil. But after seeing so much death, crime, and poverty, we had to take the risk, make a go of it, and succeed—or resign ourselves to staying the way we were.

Alvaro fell in love with the business. He cleared the land and even brought my brother to help him, with the understanding that once the money started coming in, he'd pay him the days he'd worked. They planted the seeds, my brother returned to Chaparral, and Alvaro sat down and had a good look at all he'd done. He'd get up early and, before having his coffee, go and see if any of the pods had started to bloom. He dreamed about seeing that garden in bloom, and, in his head, he'd already bought some land in Chaparral and built a three-room house on it for us to grow old in. But they were the kinds of dreams that poison you as time passes. The more you dream them, the frailer they become until you finally destroy them.

In the days just before the garden started to bloom, a group of fifteen men, some wearing uniforms and others in street clothes, came to the farm and asked me for some water. I'd never seen them before and didn't know who they were. They said they took care of the mountains in Tolima. They drank their water, keeping their backs to me and their faces hidden under their caps. Two weeks later, another group showed up. They had a couple of chickens with them and asked if I'd kill them. They also wanted me to sell them some lunch. I did, and they ate without showing me their faces, the same as the others had.

When they finished, the men came into the house and motioned Alvaro outside, saying they wanted to talk to him in private. The memory of Don Raúl came into my head, and I asked where they were taking him. I started to follow them, but they stopped me at the door. One of them put his foot out to trip me, and, just as I was stepping over it, a cold shiver ran though me like the cold that comes out of the mouth of a dead person. I couldn't move. Without looking at me, he told me to relax, that they just wanted to talk to the man of the house.

From the window I could see Alvaro by the river. He had his hands behind his back as if to tell me he had no choice in the matter and for me not to try anything because that would be the end for us. He looked like a child who was being scolded by the teacher for not doing his work. When he came back to the house, his face was white. He said, "Look, I've got to go with them to see the commander. Don't worry, they promised nothing would happen to us, to you, or the children. They want to clear things up so everyone knows what's what, and we can go back to work."

I didn't believe him and grabbed onto him around the neck. I told the guerrillas, "You aren't leaving here without me. I won't let you take him alone. Kill me if you want and be cowards for killing a woman, but you're not taking him."

The one in charge said, "That's enough. Nobody's going to do anything to anybody. If we wanted to hurt you, we wouldn't be screwing around like this. So shut up, or you'll wake up your kids."

I was so intent on Alvaro, I'd forgotten about the children.

"Take it easy, woman, we're just going to talk," Alvaro told me. Then, under his breath, he added: "They want money."

That, and thinking about the children, calmed me down a little. Had I been alone, though, I'd have gone with him, or they wouldn't have taken him. Then they started to leave. Alvaro felt better when I calmed down. I could see it in his eyes when he said goodbye. Your eyes always help when you're trying to say what you have to say. That's why the worst thing about being blind isn't that you can't see but that you can't use your eyes to talk, because that's like talking with your whole face.

The commander was stern and serious and didn't beat around the bush. "Look, every garden here pays. Everything that makes money, pays," he told Alvaro.

"We know you have five hectares. So you pay a million pesos

for every crop you bring in, whether it's good or bad, whether you sell it or not. If they pay you well, we won't say anything about it, and, if they cheat you, that's your problem. If you're not interested, you've got twenty-four hours to go. Take what you brought with you and tell Doña Maruja to find someone else. But if you plan to stay, I'll give you another warning. The paracos are around, and, if you have any dealings with them, you better kiss everything goodbye because we won't permit it. If we find out you've had anything to do with those sons-of-bitches, you're a dead man."

That's all Alvaro said they told him when he came back the next day, tired and hungry but unharmed. He didn't mention the paracos so as not to worry me. I had my doubts and fears, woman's intuition I suppose, but clung to the illusion that everything would somehow turn out all right.

The first crop was a good one. People who knew the business told Alvaro that was because we'd had plenty of water, not much wind, and the earth hadn't been overworked. I'd look over at those pretty, red flowers from a distance and began to imagine myself fixing up the house in Chaparral. The milky gum sold at a good price. But then, one night, the evil arrived. Another group of fifteen or so armed men walked up and, without so much as a greeting, called Alvaro over to them and said: "We've come for what we agreed. How much did you sell and what price did you get?"

Alvaro did the math and and told them: "Well, it's this and that but I can't pay you everything now because they haven't paid me yet. I'll pay you in two quotas."

They didn't like that and started insulting him.

"You really think we're that stupid to leave it like that?

No. You'll pay all you owe now, and you'll thank us for leaving you alive."

Alvaro had no choice. He took out what he had and handed it over to the men. They left, and we could breathe again. Another group of men came back a couple of days later. They called Alvaro over and, without another word, began tying him up. They shut me and the children in the bedroom. Alvaro began shouting: "What's the matter? What's going on? Didn't I pay you what you asked for?"

"You're making a mistake! You can't kill him!" I screamed at them. I sensed the worst and could see in their eyes they were going to kill my husband. The one in charge yelled at me: "Son-of-a-bitch, we warned you. You're working with the paras. We told you very clearly there's no dealing with them. You're working with those bastards."

That was that. They took him away like that and in my desperation I screamed and scratched my own face in rage. They wouldn't listen to anything, not our tears or our pleas or the explanations Alvaro tried to give them about how we weren't working with the paras and how they tricked us by saying they were guerrillas. Nothing. They tied him to a fence-post and shot him.

When they left, I ran to him, but he was already dead. I saw Don Raúl again in my head; it was the same face. The dead all look alike, as if at the end they all see the same thing or end up in the same place. When I came to my senses, I saw the children were there beside me overcome with tears. We made an altar to him there with our suffering and buried him in the patio of the house. The neighbors helped me, and, before he cooled off, we covered him with the same earth he'd worked, the earth where we'd planted so many hopes and dreams. Everything we had was buried with him. I left everything there. Everything.

I came here to Ibagué with my children, and we live off what I make selling *arepas* in the bus terminal. I know I am to blame and that it was my greed that led us to La Marina. Thinking we were going to have a house and a garden and that we'd be able to earn enough money for everything was the beginning of the end. But fate took over, coming like it always does from where you least expect it. The jeep and the passengers who were hurt in the accident was what made us get mixed up with amapola.

I can't and won't forgive that lady who promised us a life full of marvelous things. I'm sure she knew how we'd struggled to provide for our children, yet she didn't hesitate to send us straight into the lion's mouth. Who knows how many others she's done the same to, people like us, just trying to make a couple of million pesos, money I know she herself has no need for.

I'll never forgive the guerrillas for not trying to find out more about what happened, about our mistake. We acted in good faith. The paracos tricked us, and, what's more, they tricked the guerrillas into committing a crime. They killed an innocent person out of fear. And because they are so used to believing they're always right and that no one can disagree with them. Maybe that works with their own soldiers, but it doesn't work with ordinary people, civilians, who aren't with them. They let the paracos fool them. I don't understand how they can kill someone without even letting him speak. Sure, they told Alvaro not to have any dealings with the paracos. But how could we know the men who came for the money were paras? How could we know? Why didn't they ask for an explanation? You always end caught up in the middle of hatred you have nothing to do with. If they'd only given Alvaro a chance to speak!

I will always hate them wherever I am. They say hatred doesn't get you anywhere, that it only poisons your blood. But what can I do? Every day, when my children ask me about their father, when they're hungry or I see they don't have enough to wear or are suffering, I hate them more. I haven't said anything to my children because I don't want them to grow up looking for revenge because it will destroy their soul. The food my children don't have only increases my hatred. No child of mine ever went to bed hungry in Chaparral. And I never felt like dying so that it would all be over.

You can't imagine what it's like to listen to your child cry and cry of hunger until he's too tired to cry any longer. Or what it's like to have to divide a ten-cent piece of bread into three pieces. You start losing your will to go on living and struggling and you become a bad example for the children. Because survival is the first law of any human being, a sacred law.

Chapter 7

Osiris

I

I was born in Dabeiba, but I was brought up
in the Palo Alto hamlet. My father was a
campesino who knew the land. It was his life.
He built a sugar press by himself, so he could
make *guarapo,* honey, and *panela,* and he
had some coffee bushes and planted cocoa
and corn. We liked to watch him because
you could see he enjoyed his work and was
grateful to have it. He was a man who wasn't
afraid to sweat and, because of that, we had
everything we needed. Today you'd call it

abundance—we had all we needed and then some.

He lost a lot during the violence of the 1950s and that troubled him. He had to send us away and go it alone, so we'd have enough to eat. He ended up losing his land as well, and going to Apartadó to work on someone else's land. There were fifteen of us in those days, five dead and ten alive. Children are a poor man's old-age security. We lived well until that time, but then things started going bad. My father wasn't allowed to sell more than a certain amount each day, and only at the price the farm bosses said. And if that wasn't humiliating enough, you had to act like you were grateful all the time.

That combination of work and the sadness that came with it started taking its toll on my father, and he fell sick. His complexion started to yellow, he got weaker and stopped sleeping, and he lost his appetite. When a working man like him stops eating, it's like he's already dead, and it wasn't long before we buried him.

We started pig farming, bringing pigs in from Ituango to fatten up and kill, then sell as *chicharrón* here in town. Apartadó has always been full of Antioqueños, and they love their pork. I worked cleaning houses, and every kind of leftover I could find, whether it was clothes or food, I'd take home to my brothers and sisters. My mother was sick. She'd had an operation, and they'd done it badly, and she couldn't do much to help.

As we grew older, we began to get tired of staying around the house, and everyone started going their own way. Sometimes, it seemed none of us could get along at all. I still worked fattening the pigs, my own pigs, and washing people's clothes, so I could pay for my younger brothers and sisters to go to school. Some days the cupboard had nothing in it, and we'd have to give the kids a stick and a hook so they could go fishing in the river. I never did any studying myself, but I'm proud I helped all my brothers and sisters learn to read and write. Sometimes, when things were going badly, a black storekeeper named Don Julio would give us a hand. He'd tell me, "Osiris, when you don't have anything to cook, you come over here."

I would, and he'd give me whatever he could. There were days when I'd come home with a basket of food on my head, and the kids would show up with a string of fish. That's how we ate.

Don Julio became my fiancé without me even knowing it, and one day he told me we were going to get married. He was well off and, in addition to having the store, worked as secretary to the town's judge. He bought me a new dress for the wedding, some shoes, and a bow for my hair, but when I saw all those presents, I got scared. A lady told me another black woman was pregnant with Don Julio's child, and I was afraid she'd put a spell on me. My friends also told me I was much too young for him and that if I married him things would get difficult. Well, they convinced me, and I told Don Julio I wanted to stop seeing him. He told me he loved me, but my mind was made up. To get rid of him, I wrote a letter to myself and signed it with his woman's name. It said that if I married him I'd have to pay. I showed it to him and then used it the best I could, saying I couldn't put myself in that situation, that I'd never done anything to her, and so on. Well, he cried and cried over me, but that was that. He sent me notes and letters and presents, but I left him for good. In spite of the fact he could help support us, I couldn't get the fear of the spell out of my head, and I stayed as poor as I'd always been.

I met the man who would be the father of my first children three months later. My family didn't want him in the house because he was a cowboy who worked from farm to farm without anything steady. I saw him for the first time at my cousin's house, and I liked how he looked as he worked the horses. He started to flirt and come after me, but at first I didn't want to have anything to do with him. I'd tell him, "Don't follow me around, man. This Black girl doesn't want any of that!"

I'd tell him I didn't like him, and he'd say, *"That suits me fine because I know how to tame young fillies."*

I felt good around that boy. He was seventeen, elegant, and fine looking. But my mother didn't like him, less because of his age and more because he was broke. That old saying about the forbidden fruit being the most attractive one proved to be the case, and I fell in love with him to spite my mother. You don't fall in love with someone but against someone. They wouldn't let me bring him in the house, and we had to visit out on the street under a mango tree. I'd take a chair out there to cool off and sit waiting for him. As soon as he'd mention them not letting him in the house, I'd say, "No, they don't like you. That's the way it is."

He wouldn't let that stop him and ask, "But you love me, don't you?"

I'd lie and say no. Then he began saying we could go away together and get married.

"No, sir. You think you can just come out and ask me something like that? Who do you think you are?"

That was how the conversation went every day, him saying we should leave together and me refusing and playing hard to get. My mother, meanwhile, never passed up the chance to remind me that I'd let Don Julio get away. Now there was a good man, she'd say. The husband I needed and so on. Until one day, I'd had enough and told her, "You know what, mama? No one is going to buy me. I'll go with whoever I want because I like them. Julio works for the government and that appeals to you, but it doesn't appeal to me. If I fall in love with an imbecile, that's who my husband will be!"

Well, she slapped my face, and I can still feel its sting to this day. God, I was a mouthy girl! I said, "Now you'll see who I really am!"

The next time he asked me to go away with him, I said, "Fine. Get me everything a woman who lives in your house needs, and let's go."

Eladio was a hard worker and lined up a house right away. He left the morning of July 16, 1964, and came back that same night with everything ready.

"So fast?" I asked him.

"Everything is ready. All that's missing is you."

But I wasn't so sure anymore and thought that once he had me he'd end up leaving me. Because men are very anxious to conquer you, especially if you're pretty. Sometimes I think they go after pretty women not so much because they like them, but so their friends can admire them. They get women for other men to look at. I told him all this but none of it bothered him. He listened to me as if he were listening to the rain. I finished by saying that if I left my house, I wasn't going back. In a slow, serious voice he said, "No, Osiris. Don't even think like that. You're a very capable and hard-working woman. Why would I ever treat you like that?"

He knew I was up pounding corn every morning before dawn and that I worked until midnight grinding it and making *arepas*. He got up early to round up the cows to milk and knew what I did because he'd look through a crack in the kitchen wall at me when he went by. He admired me for working like that and that made me feel proud of myself. He'd say he wanted to take me away, not to make me do more, but so I could have some free time.

I knew he understood how hard I worked at home. But I also knew that more than loving me, he wanted me. I had long hair hanging down below my waist, and I used to wear it in braids. When he'd look at me with his glassy, half-closed eyes, I'd feel a mixture of pleasure and fear. And then he'd lick his lips and say he couldn't wait to undo my braids and caress the "lion's mane." I didn't like when he said that, but when he looked at me like that, I'd almost melt. I had to watch myself, so he wouldn't see how weak it made me feel, so I'd say, "That's a nice story. But unless you get serious you won't be getting to know any lion, braids or no braids!"

He'd insist he had loved me since the first time he saw me. "Sure, sure," I'd say. "First time? What are you talking about, the first time?"

"Look, that time when you were carrying a huge pile of clothes to wash. It was so heavy you couldn't manage, and I helped you carry them."

He was right. I remembered seeing him that day come riding up on a colt, a sorrel I liked more than its rider. Well, after that story, I told him right there I'd go with him, but it had to be soon. There was so much to do at home. There were four women—my sisters, my mother, and me—the rest were men and youngsters, and it was up to me to make enough to feed and clothe the ones that were at school. I'd also go to work in the fields whenever I heard they were looking for someone to swing a machete. If there was a corn harvest and they were paying well, that's where I'd be. I could work as hard as any man.

I told Eladio I was ready to go with him but that I didn't love

him. A woman doesn't admit her love outright like that. He said
fine, and I told him to come by my house at night, and I'd be
waiting. Well, that night I lay there waiting for him, acting like I
was asleep. My mother slept beside me, and she was a light sleeper.
And we had a guard dog that barked at his own shadow, so,
when Eladio arrived at eleven, his yapping woke everyone up. I
had all my clothes folded neatly in a box—I've never liked wrinkled dresses—so I picked it up quietly, opened the door, and left.

We met up on the main road. He took the box from me and
said we'd better get going. It was safe in those days, and you
could be out walking all night and nothing would happen to you.
Eladio was almost eighteen. I don't know how old I was because
I'd never paid any attention to the years as they passed by. My
life was just work. I didn't even know when I turned fifteen. I
complained to my mother about not knowing my age because
you have to tell your children how old they are. I never knew
when I was born, and I only got my *cédula* after my husband
died so I could claim his body.

As we were passing a farm, I decided to test Eladio and told
him I was going back. He grabbed my hand hard and said, "No,
missy! You left with me and from here on you are mine."

I answered, "I don't think so! No sir. No one's bought and
sold me. Give me my box now!"

"I'll give you the box but not your clothes. I'll take them
back to your mother tomorrow and, while I'm there, tell her just
what I think."

His talking like that made me mad, and I got as angry and
aggressive as a cat in heat. When we got to the house he'd set up,
I didn't want to go in. He was still going on about me being his,
and I was saying I didn't belong to anybody. I was sorry I'd ever

left my house and figured I was probably crazy. But better to be
crazy behind closed doors than in the street, so I went in.

It was a big house, well-built, and he'd fixed the bedroom up
nicely. Well, I sat down on the bed, and that's where I stayed until
the next morning. I was still angry at him, and, whenever he'd
tell me to lie down, I said I wasn't tired. He finally fell asleep,
and I sat there all night, crying and thinking how my mother
and my family were all going to hate me.

He got up early, made coffee, and before leaving for work,
told me I was the woman of the house and had to decide what to
do with everything there. I didn't know what to do because all
my life I'd worked for everything I had. I grew up living from
day to day and, like any poor person, got used to doing without.
I had no idea what to ask him for. He came back about nine
with some groceries and a box with shoes in it and pieces of
material I could use to have some dresses made.

I'd always lived in a small house with a big family. Now, all
of a sudden I had a big house and a little family. Everything was
upside down and the loneliness of an empty house is a heavy
weight to bear. It was just the two of us living there in El Tigre, a
town up above Chigorodó. Eladio loved me and showed me he
loved me in many ways. He would give to me in a way I wasn't
used to receiving. With only Eladio to take care of, housework
was easy for me.

Eladio was good with cattle and had no trouble finding work
on the big haciendas. He'd be gone for days. I was so naïve! He
had a girlfriend, and he'd bring her home with him. He told me
it was so she could keep me company, so I wouldn't be so lonely.
They'd play around in bed, and I'd make them food and take it
in to them there. I didn't think there was anything more than

friendship between the two of them.

Well, some of the older women neighbors told me she was my husband's lover. But I didn't get it. Then they explained it more clearly and I understood. But I kept defending them anyway, so the women wouldn't all see how stupid I was. She was a very dangerous woman, that one, and we women know what that means, to be a dangerous woman. He started up with her because he knew I wouldn't catch on. It never occurred to me a married man would have anything to do with another woman. To me, marriage was a man with his woman and nothing else.

When I came to my senses and realized my life wasn't what I thought it was, I became a wild woman. I'd go after another woman and knock her down without thinking twice. He had to hide the machete from me. Words don't fix those kinds of things, and more than one of his ladyfriends got a nice surprise from me when she came calling. After that, they all got scared of me and would hide when they saw me coming. Eladio laughed at it all.

I ended up pregnant after one of those arguments. I didn't really understand what that meant, but an older lady neighbor of mine explained it to me.

After my baby girl was born, I decided to wait three months and then leave Eladio. He said I wouldn't be any better off leaving because he'd go after me wherever I went. Then he said we should get married. Who understands men? They say they're crazy about you and can't live without you one minute and then begin acting just the opposite. I said no because of the way he'd treated me and because I didn't want that bitterness to ruin my life. We should just leave things the way they were, I told him. I had my baby and that was that. I sure wasn't going to marry him and then have him go back to his girlfriends. He could forget that, because I'd just as soon kill any one of them.

Well, he promised he'd change after that, and he did. He began to be kind and considerate and spoiled me whenever he had the chance. He was the one who told those women goodbye. We had all we needed at home and began to feel as a family should. I started thinking I didn't want my little girl to suffer if I could help it and tried to change too. We never got married, but we did stay together and had six children, three girls and three boys. As time passed, I tried not to bother Eladio, and he began spending weekends out of the house, leaving on Saturday and coming back on Monday. When he'd get back, I'd ask if he was thirsty and fix him a strong lemonade. Then, under his breath, he'd say, "Negra, have you got anything else?"

And, since I'd be expecting the question, I'd serve him some leftovers I always put aside for him.

I had no complaints, and things changed between us. He started staying home Saturdays and became quieter. I saw the change in him, and the fear he felt of losing me and of losing our home together. We lived thirteen years like that until they killed him.

II

In a way, I guess you could say it was only a matter of time. Eladio had a cousin named Aristi who'd been a real bad kid when he was young, and neither of us liked him coming so often to the house. I didn't because I'd heard he was a *matón*, a killer, or at least had been, and Eladio didn't because he'd probably seen him do something during one of those times I'd heard about. There was even a rumor Aristi had killed some kids. I don't know about that, but he sure scared me. He was a man running from the sins of his past. Maybe it was remorse that made him follow us around so much, but whenever we went anywhere, he'd show up. He was a lonely man.

The last day, Eladio told me he felt like eating a *sancocho de gallina.* I kept some hens because I knew that was one of his favorite dishes. Anyway, I killed one of them and began cooking the sancocho. We had a small garden out back planted with onions, cilantro, and some other herbs, and I was picking what I needed for the sauce when Aristi showed up, and everything went bad.

Eladio said he was probably hungry and told me to give him something, and I served him some sancocho. I had put our ten-month-old girl in a box on the floor in the kitchen, so she wouldn't follow me out of the house, and I remember Eladio crouching down and spooning some soup into her mouth.

Just then, I saw a couple of men approaching the house. There was something strange about them, and I told Eladio to look at them. People used to talk about "La Mano Negra" in those days—a group of killers for hire—and the men made us think of them. They came to the door and said,

"Good afternoon. Is Mr. Aristi here?"

"No," said Eladio, who had gone out to talk to them.

I don't know why he lied. Maybe he sensed the evil they brought with them. That was my husband's mistake. The blood drained from my face, and I walked over to block the kitchen door so they wouldn't see Aristi sitting there eating at the table. The men said they knew he was in the house. I told them to look elsewhere because there was no one in there except my daughter. All of a sudden, one of them shoved me away from the door. Aristi stood up and said, "Here I am. What can I do for you?"

That's the way he was: direct, as if he were angry. Well, both men took out their guns and started shooting. I screamed for my child because she was inside the box there in the kitchen beside Aristi. But I couldn't move. It was as if I knew what was going to happen had already happened. Eladio sprang to pick up his daughter. The killers thought he was going after them, and one of them pointed his gun straight at him and shot him in the head. He turned to look at me and said, "Look, Negra. They killed me!"

Everything happened at once. I watched Eladio fall to the floor as if he were falling in slow motion, and my world was falling with him. I couldn't hear anything. I couldn't speak. I just watched him falling … falling … falling … until he went down like a big tree that's been cut down. I lost control and began screaming. The children were crying. My little girl was covered in blood, and my two older ones were clinging to my dress. I couldn't hear what they were screaming. I didn't hear anything. All I remember is what one of the killers said before he left: "Don't cry so much, you're still young."

Eladio asked for something to drink as he lay dying, and I gave him a little water from a spoon. I lay him on my lap in the middle of all that blood but I stopped myself from crying because I didn't want him to know he was dying. Then I went outside and sat down in the street and screamed. Screamed and heard my own terrible screams! I wanted to run away, but I didn't have the nerve to leave the two dead men alone there. Or the nerve to go back into the kitchen and see their cold eyes. I didn't know what to do or who to call. Everything became quiet. A breeze started to blow … everything was still, everything began to slip away.

I was thinking about what would become of me alone with four small children when I looked up and saw one of Aristi's brothers. He never had any use for his brother and was always after him because of the bad things he had done. When I told him they'd killed both of them, he replied, "I can see that."

He left to find a truck in town to take the bodies away and bury them. What else can you do with a body that's already cold? About seven that night, he came back with the police inspector. My oldest child, Blanca, who was ten, was in shock from seeing so much death, and she asked me over and over to put something in the hole in her father so it would stop bleeding.

I felt as if Eladio's death had ripped something out of me without knowing what it was. But it hurt. It hurt so much. Thinking of my children hurt me. If I gave them clothes, I wouldn't be able to give them food; if I gave them food, they'd have to do without clothes. Staying alive was like a death sentence. Were the children I had that were still alive going to die on me? I'd already had to bury two of my children. They both died before being baptized. But dying that way isn't the same as being killed. Not for you, and not for the one who dies. Maybe to God it's the same. The oldest lived until he was three. Then the parasites got him and took him away. The other was born *descuajado,* with his stomach and insides detached. We took him to a good doctor, but he died anyway. He lived thirteen months. I was twenty-five years old, and I had four children alive and two already dead.

I was thinking about all that when they came for the bodies. The oldest boy was fighting and pleading with his father to wake up, so they wouldn't take him away, and they had to pull him off Eladio.

The police inspector began taking measurements with a bricklayer's tape measure and asked who the dead men were. Then he asked who killed them and why. As he talked, he

measured and measured. I couldn't figure out what all the meas-
uring was for if the dead were already dead. As he rolled the
bodies over and over, he asked again who had done it, but I
didn't know anything about that.

"The ones in La Mano Negra," I said.

"To prejudge is a crime. Widow or no widow, you have no
reason to make false accusations," he replied.

He made me swear I'd tell the truth, then asked again who
the killers were, how they were dressed, and how old they were.
I said I didn't know their ages because I hadn't asked them, that
they were wearing pants and a shirt like everyone else. I couldn't
describe them any better because they looked the same as everyone else. In my mind, I could see them shooting and remember
how they fired. But I couldn't describe what they looked like. I
couldn't bring myself to remember any more about that moment,
as if I were afraid of losing Eladio's final minute of life.

The police inspector stared at me with anger on his face, the
anger you use to hide your fear. He didn't know whether I was
telling the truth. I can still see his expression and feel his animosity
towards me. It wasn't until much later that I found out what he
was afraid of.

He told someone to put the bodies in the back of the truck,
and they threw them in like a couple of dead pigs. We got in there,
too, and my boy lay down by his father, hugging him and talking quietly in his ear as we drove. I couldn't find the words to tell
him to stop talking to his father, to tell him he was already dead.

They did the autopsies, and we held the wake in the dead
men's house, as it should be. Thoughts crowded into my head—
thoughts more than feelings—and I began to feel like a chicken
that's been cornered to kill and make a soup with. I didn't know

what to do next. If I did one thing, I told myself, I couldn't do another. I couldn't sleep after that, and I stopped eating. I spent all my time sitting on the bed with a flashlight in one hand and a pack of cigarettes in the other. And a box of matches and coffee. I drank coffee, smoked, and cried.

Three months passed that way. I was all skin and bones. I'd pick up a cup, and my hand would shake. I could hardly take care of myself, and I'd all but forgotten my children. The neighbors looked after us and brought us food to cook, and Blanca fed me.

Then one day a neighbor came in and demanded to know what I was doing with my life. Was I just going to let the sadness drag me under, she asked me. If I was going to let myself die, she'd take care of the children. I was nursing Carmencita, the youngest, but my breasts were so dry and shrivelled up that she seemed to be dying anyway. I had nothing to give her. That's when I decided to try again and take care of myself, so I could take care of my children. They were what drew me out of the black hole Eladio left me in.

I began to look for something I could do to stop being so consumed by sadness. You can get used to that and get comfortable with the tears, and that's wrong. I felt the danger in that like the aftertaste of death. I started fattening up more pigs to sell and got some chickens. I started to eat better and take vitamins. I started to live again. It was a slow process and took many days.

I began making meals and taking them to the sawyers. The hills were full of them, and I'd walk and walk looking for the wooden tables they'd set up to cut the wood. I did that for a long time until I got tired, tired of climbing up and down those mountains, even though I was making enough to take care of my children. So I decided to try my luck in the *bananeras*, the banana plantations in Apartadó. It is a hot town that stinks of the poisons they use to kill banana blight, and it's full of *sicarios*. But that's where the money was.

I looked up one of my sisters there and, through her, met Señora Yoya, who took me to one of the bananeras that needed workers. I told the man in charge that Yoya and I were family and he said, "Good. Be here at six tomorrow morning. That's when we divide up the workers."

Well, at six sharp, there I was, wearing a dress I'd been saving for years for a special occasion. When they asked if I knew how to pack fruit, I told them the truth. I didn't. But I said I was a fast learner and I'd come to learn.

They sent me off with a fellow to teach me, and I was all ears and eyes that afternoon. They took me a box to see what I'd learned like a test in school. All the workers there are jealous, and there's a lot of evil in their jealousy. I got the box and packed it carefully—as if I were packing a baby—and I did fine. So well, they thought I'd worked packing before. No, sir, the only thing I'd ever packed were my suitcases. But when God made women, he gave us the ability to fit things in tightly and well. You can see that when a baby is born! I worked there all week and went by my sister's house on Saturday to pick up my clothes. I started work again the next day, because in the bananeras Sunday's a regular work day, not a holiday.

I packed bananas there for two weeks and when I got my first pay, I took the money and ran out to buy groceries for the children. They were living with my mother in the house where their father was killed.

I tell you, this negra waltzed in there, and people took notice! It was plain for everyone to see I'd started a new life for myself and my children. Things hadn't started to go bad yet in those days. The *sicarios* were around, and sometimes you'd see the guns in their packs and the evil in their eyes, and you'd be afraid. But I'd say to myself, if I don't do anything to anyone, no one will do anything to me. How naive I was!

My pay was thirty thousand pesos, but, even so, it wasn't enough for all of us to eat. All the same, Eladio had been dead for two years, and I was slowly beginning to leave the sadness behind me. I was working, looking after myself and my family, and the days passed by. There were no men in my life, only work and family.

I packed bananas on that farm for eighteen months. One day, a couple of young guys arrived looking for work. They were from Caquetá, happy-go-lucky types but hard workers, and, when the boss saw that, he hired them. Work in the bananeras is hard, really hard, and not everybody can tough it out. But those two really knew how to work.

Well, the youngest of them took an interest in me right from the start. That I was older and a widow with children didn't bother him a bit. I told him I didn't even want to talk about any of that, that I'd been through it all and it was all ancient history. I told him to go after the younger girls, the ones without kids and obligations. But he insisted so much—Milciades was his name—and was so determined that I ended up giving in and we lived together for twelve years.

I'll always think of Milciades as a boy even though he's forty-two and I'm fifty-five. We had two boys together, and, when everything seemed to be going well between us, I moved my whole family to live with us in Apartadó. Life was good. We worked on the same farm and made enough between us to buy something for everybody. Then I found out he had a younger woman. She had four kids but hadn't lived nearly as much as I had.

I realized things don't always happen as you think they should. A wife should end up burying her husband and not the other way around. But that's just what I was afraid was going to happen. I told Milciades that if he was so fond of her, he should leave my children alone. And if he loved her, he should leave me. But I also said I needed money from him to feed and school the kids he'd given me. I felt he no longer thought of me as a good woman. But he told me just the opposite. He said you couldn't make a better woman than me if you tried. Even with those problems, though, I made up my mind not to be bitter and tried to make his life as pleasant as I could.

All I finally asked was that he leave before I became bitter. We both knew those twelve years had been good ones, loving ones, and that gratitude wasn't going to turn into bitterness. I knew I was going to suffer, but I didn't want to stand in his way. I knew we could stay friends. In all, I worked for four years on the farm where we met and managed to make enough to buy a small lot in the Policarpa barrio. He worked there for ten years, and they gave him seven million pesos when they let him go. He never gave me a peso of that money, and our two children lived in the house I built on the lot. The youngest would get a call from his father every once in a blue moon and maybe some clothes; the oldest never got anything, not even the time of day.

The oldest began to help me by selling "chance," lottery tickets. That's what you do when you don't know how to do anything else, and it's the last hope of all those who are losing even that. I'd always set aside enough to buy a ticket once we'd bought the food we needed. We lived off the money we made from selling *empanadas, morcillas,* and *arepas.* We made them, and the kids sold them in the street, and we'd pay for the water and electricity in the house with what they brought back. Blanca helped a great deal, and we lived well enough.

I never got over my feelings for Milciades, though, and deep down I still hurt. My children had grown up in the twelve years we lived together, and he never shirked his responsibilities as their father. I am a strong person, and I've become even stronger by facing what I've had to face. But there are some things in my life I don't think I could have managed alone. Fate brought me two men, and I grabbed on to both of them for support during difficult times, times I wanted to die myself. Eladio consoled me when my two children died, and Milciades cried with me when we buried Jaime, the oldest boy I had with Eladio. He watched Jaime grow up and took his body to the cemetery after he was killed.

There is a park in Apartadó called the Parque Infantil. Jaime was nineteen. He worked as a watchman and had a small house, a woman, and a baby. He wasn't a drinker and was a good boy. One day, a couple of his friends stopped by his work and invited him out for a couple of drinks. I'd always doted on him, and he stopped by the house first to tell me he was going out for a couple of rums. The times were beginning to change for the worse, and I told him to be careful. I didn't want him to drink too much because, as a mother, you have feelings that tell you when something bad is going to happen. His friends were waiting for him in the bar.

Without us ever knowing why, soldiers arrived, pulled them out of the bar, blindfolded them with their own shirts and took them to the Parque Infantil. People saw what happened, but, in those days, everybody was too scared to say anything to anyone.

They shot the older ones first. As a watchman, my son had a pistol, and, when he tried to pull it out, they shot him. One of the bullets hit his hand and went into his waist, another went into his stomach, and the last one into his face. He died right away, but the others died a horrible death. The soldiers were angry and shot them over and over. I knew right away it was the army. I knew. My heart told me.

Jaime always came by the house at six in the morning after finishing his shift. He'd have coffee and then head home to his woman. I was getting the children's clothes ready for school at six thirty when I heard a car stop in front of the house. I went outside and they asked me if I was Jaime's mother. I felt the cold hand of death take hold of me again and asked what happened to my son.

"They killed him at dawn," was the answer.

Oh my God! My blessed God! How empty I felt! How I longed to die with my son! Maybe God understands what He does but how can we? I got into the car the way I was—I didn't even notice I had slippers on—and when we got to the hospital, Blanca was there, screaming they'd killed her brother. They took us to the morgue. The killings had started, and it was full of bodies.

"Look for him," one of the military doctors told me, motioning over to some large sinks where bodies were piled one on top of the other. "Over there with the ones they brought in this morning," he added, his voice full of authority. There were men and women there; some were complete, others were in pieces. I walked over and began to lift them up by their hair, so I could see their faces. All the while I kept saying there had to be some mistake, that my son couldn't be among all these bodies.

"Go into the next room and look at the ones in the corner,"

the man yelled.

And, yes, there they were, the ones from the park. They were in their underwear and hadn't been cleaned up. When I saw my son, I felt the world fall away from me. I lifted him up and held him against my chest. The doctor, or whoever he was, told me not to touch him, that it could implicate me in the investigation, but I didn't listen to him. I hugged my boy against me, and his blood, his precious blood, ran all over me until that animal—half-doctor, half-policeman—pulled him away from me.

I felt as if I were going crazy and went out into the street screaming. Where do you demand justice when the authorities who pick up the bodies are the same ones who kill them? Who do you denounce the crime to if the authorities are all smeared with blood? The same people who take the measurements and do the tests to see who the killer is are the ones who committed the crime. I knew because I had already lived through it, and that's what I told the doctors or whoever they were to their faces. I sat down on the street there and cried and screamed until a captain walked over and told me my son had a gun. I heard him but couldn't say anything because I felt something blocking my throat. When I could speak, I said why wouldn't he have a gun if he was a watchman. Then he started asking me questions and acting as if he didn't know what had happened. He wanted to know who killed him. I stared at him—stared at him to humiliate him—and yelled, "You must know how you did it! You're the one who gave the order to kill him, and now you want to know what happened?"

He walked away, angry at how I'd answered. When he came back a while later, there was a captain in civilian clothes with him, and they continued their questions: who had done it, how, how did I know who it was, who told me? They wrote down everything I said. That's how I got mixed up in the investigation. They use the law to do what they can't do with their guns, and I gave it all to them on a platter. The same ones who committed the crime ended up investigating it, and the one they investigated was the dead man's family—me.

My emotions boiled over. I asked for my son's body and took him away. I wanted to have the wake in his house. They went to the farm to get Milciades because he loved that boy and had taken him in very young and brought him up. He came and made the arrangements. That happened on May 8, 1990, two days before one of my daughters disappeared.

She had just turned sixteen years old. I don't know the details of her death, though, and I could never find out for sure what happened. She's the only one who knows that—she and the men who killed her. She'd gone out with some of her friends on the sixth, and, when they left her, she was on her way home. Later, after we'd buried Jaime and some time had passed, a man told me they'd killed her just outside Apartadó in a place called Nueva Antioquia. He said he saw them pulling a girl like mine off a *buseta* and then killing her there. I asked him who'd done it, and he said the only people around there at that moment were the police. But that's all he'd say. I can't be sure either. Of my son's death, yes, because I saw him, and I buried him. But my daughter? I can't even say for sure whether she's dead or not. I am still waiting for her. If my girl's dead, she's been dead for as long as my boy. I know she left the house with only the clothes she was wearing because the rest of her things are still at home. Sometimes I have the feeling that maybe she's still alive, that she went off with a man and is all right. Or went away with a friend of hers or is just out there somewhere. That's how I try to think of her. That's the hope I have.

I've loved all my children the same, and I've been the same mother to all of them. I chewed their food for them before they had teeth, and I was there to comfort them when they cried. I've always been the same mother to all of them, and it scares me that they're being killed. I don't want to bury my children.

Everything ended for me after they killed Jaime and my little girl disappeared. I am alive, but I'm not living a life anymore. I became an old woman that morning and the mother of two murdered children. And in my loneliness I was alone. People from the barrio began being killed. They'd go off to work and never come back. Then show up two or three days later with their mouths full of flies. You'd hear people say: We saw so many of them with their faces covered on such and such a street last night and, the next morning, the dead would appear and the living would disappear. No one was safe. That's when we first heard of the paracos.

I'd never heard the word before and didn't know what it meant. I didn't ask too many questions either because the captain was still investigating. Better to be quiet, even though my silence only made me hurt more inside. I didn't want anyone else to be killed and didn't even care if they told me who had killed my son and "disappeared" my daughter. I already knew who was responsible. Knew as a mother knows. It was that knowledge that brought them after me. They broke into my house looking for me, and I wasn't going to wait for it to happen again. I left the house we'd built in Policarpa.

I'd left Apartadó and was on my way to Dabeiba the first time they came for me. My youngest daughter, Carmen, was alone in the house with her younger brother. They were in bed when they saw a group of men, big men with crewcuts, in the other room.

They didn't look like they were from Apartadó and had a couple
of men wearing hoods with them. They didn't knock or anything, just burst right into the bedroom. Carmen woke up with
their flashlights shining in her eyes. She sat up, rubbed her eyes,
and asked who they were. They said they were from DAS or
from F2. I don't remember. She said they had no right to be
there, that they could've broken the door coming in like that,
and hadn't they ever been to school and learned any manners.

"What's that?" they said menacingly. "Are you saying we're
louts?"

They insulted her and began searching the house but Carmen
didn't let them out of her sight. They asked where I was—that's
who they were after—and Carmen told them I was in Medellín.
They told her not to move while they searched the other rooms.
But Carmen wasn't born yesterday and figured if they had the
chance they'd plant something in the house and then accuse us.
So she stuck right with them, following them room to room,
until they left. Then she sat down on the stoop outside and
waited for the dawn.

At five the next morning she went to Blanca's house—she
lived in the same barrio—and told her what happened. They'd
done the same thing to her and to a number of other families in
Policarpa that night. Blanca is full of fire, and, when the men
entered her house, she told them what she thought with a string
of insults that stopped them dead in their tracks. They'd never
heard a woman talk like that. They searched her house anyway,
and when they saw her back door ajar, said someone must have
left just before they arrived. That made her even angrier because
it wasn't true and because the men never told her who they were
looking for.

When I got back and heard what happened, I moved out. I put a lock on the door and took my children to sleep with a friend. They came back that same night, broke the lock, and trashed the house. They threw all the pots and pans and plates on the kitchen floor along with the pictures we had in the bedroom, and took everything out of the clothes basket. The next day, one of the neighbors told me she'd seen policemen there as well, some of them with their faces covered, and said they'd been looking for me. Someone else who'd seen them told me the ones with their faces covered were soldiers.

After that, I had no choice but to leave the house for good, and, with it, all the work and time I'd put into it. I left the keys with one of the neighbors in the hopes she could rent it and moved in with a friend in downtown Apartadó. The situation in town was getting worse, and it wasn't just happening to me but to more and more people.

The people who lived in Policarpa were working-class people, and more and more of them were leaving, abandoning the barrio. That was something that hurt us. We didn't know why some people considered us their enemies. We'd never stolen anything or killed anyone and couldn't understand why we were being forced into a corner like that. Neither my friend nor I could go back into Policarpa because they were looking for us. We'd ask ourselves why, but we couldn't come up with any reason. They'd already done what they wanted to me: they'd killed my son and taken away my daughter. What else were they after?

But it was when I heard they were looking for my other boy too, the oldest, that I really panicked and started running. Carlos was fifteen and worked on the *busetas* making change. At that time, Carmen was seventeen and had moved in with a fellow named Jackman. He was a good-natured boy she'd known since she was a child, and they'd rented a house outside of Currulao. Well, the day they arrived to move in, they killed Jackman. Six or seven men arrived, pulled him out of the house, and shot him right there in front of Carmen. One of my brothers used to live nearby, and, when he heard the shots, he thought they'd both been killed. When he got there, though, Carmen was crouched down on the ground sobbing. The killers asked if he was family and told him to get her out of there. He did, and, as they left, the men started shooting again at the body as it lay there. Carmen made the long trip back to Apartadó to tell me that what had happened to me had happened to her. She arrived crying, and it hurt me so much because I knew what it was like to have your husband killed in front of you, and you're unable to do anything. It hurt me to see my little girl suffering like that. We went to tell Jackman's family about it, and the next day took the body to Mutatá.

It began to get dangerous for Carlos, my fifteen-year-old, as well. I couldn't understand why so many people around me were being killed. It was turning us all into nervous wrecks because it wasn't just me. If that had been the case, then okay, I'd let them kill me, and that would be the end of it. But, no, there were killings everywhere. Everyone had someone to grieve and to mourn, and we all had stories of how so and so had been killed and what time they'd killed him. The worst of it, though, was we all knew who the killers were, but there was no one to tell because no one would do anything about it. There were shootings all the time, especially around dawn. Everyone would shut their doors until it stopped, then go out to see how many were dead and who they were. Sometimes the shooting would start at five in the morning, calm down during the day, and then start up again in the afternoon or at night. The noise was so loud it was like the world was coming to an end. There were always more shots than bodies, but then you'd see the bodies and how many bullet holes were in each.

The El Golazo massacre, for example, was horrible. It was Easter Wednesday, and I was in church with my family, praying for the souls of the dead, and, when the shooting started, we all stayed put, lying one on top of the other on the church floor. Someone said the shots were coming from Doña Melba's place. The shooting went on for half an hour, but there was no sign of the police or the army, even though they'd been around earlier checking IDs.

People who saw what happened said they were there five minutes before the shooting started and that a couple of minutes after they left, a truck pulled up, and men got out firing. When the shooting stopped, we went out to have a look. The brother of one of my friends was the first one we saw, full of holes and bleeding in the doorway. We walked on to the El Golazo discotheque, and that's where they were: thirteen bodies, a boy who sold chance and a woman who sold empanadas among them. The rest were all workers from the bananeras. No one said anything. Someone sent for the police, but they never arrived. They were probably too ashamed to even show up. There were massacres every day after that, and they became as common as the killings had been. So many massacres, but the ugliest of them was El Golazo.

I had no choice but to send my children away to the capital, Bogotá. One of my friends pawned a stereo he had and gave me the money. I raffled off a gold chain I'd had since living with Eladio, and the lady who rented the place I lived in gave me something as well. All told, I had ninety thousand pesos, enough for Carlos and Carmen to get away. Even if it meant I'd never see them again, I wanted them far away and safe, not close to me and dead. That was in 1996. I sent them off to Bogotá and stayed with the youngest.

When they got on the bus out of Apartadó, I just stood there crying. I was afraid they were going to be killed on the trip and sad I couldn't give them more money to buy food with. In Bogotá, they moved in with a woman whose husband was in jail for La Chinita.* I only knew three of the ones involved in all that, and I knew they'd been unjustly accused. Fernando was a construction foreman when I met him in Policarpa. I knew Belarmino from a bananera and know that on the night of the massacre his wife was in labor. I was with him as he waited for his child to be born. The other one, Camila, was a friend of Carmen's who'd been recently widowed. That night she'd gone to the party there to try to get herself back together again. Well, they arrested Camila and another girl, and they're all in jail in Bogotá now. The women followed the men out of the barrio. Those that stayed started getting threats and eventually left. One of them came to my house and said she had no choice but to leave because some men she didn't know were asking after her, and she was sure it was to kill her. She went one night, without a good-bye to me or anyone else.

They'd put threats under the doors where the others lived: "We'll give you so many hours to leave the region." The threats always had the person's name on them and how many hours they

---

* A 1994 FARC massacre, killing 35, in the La Chinita neighborhood of Apartadó, that was widely condemned. The attack targeted sympathizers of the Hope, Peace and Freedom movement, including trade unionists. Hope, Peace and Freedom was created as a legal political movement by demobilized guerrillas of the People's Liberation Army (EPL).

had to leave. That never changed, and they were all written in the same place by the same person.

A month later, my children told me they were coming back to Apartadó, and I began to die all over again. The peace I had knowing that I'd saved at least two of them ended. They suffered a great deal here in Bogotá. They only had two thin sheets each with them when they arrived. But sheets you use when it's hot, not blankets, and they had to put one on the ground to sleep on. They slept huddled up against each other to keep warm. And even though the woman of the house was kind, sometimes a whole day would pass without her saying a word to them, and they felt bad. They didn't have jobs and couldn't contribute anything, and, one night, they left without saying anything to her. A month passed without any word from them. I had no idea where they'd gone or what they were doing. Then one day I learned Carlos had found work in a garage and Carmen was working in a house taking care of a widower. They pleaded with me not to go back to Policarpa and said it would be better if I joined them in Bogotá.

I didn't tell them how bad things had gotten in Apartadó so as not to worry them. They were looking for me and my friend everywhere, saying they were going to kill all of the barrio's *viejas*—the longtime residents—once and for all. They said it was because we'd seen and heard a lot of things. Too many things. And I didn't even know which things I wasn't supposed to have seen or heard. But we didn't talk much about any of that because we felt we knew what the problem was. At first, I thought I could hang on. But the two threats and the times they broke into my house were enough for me. I probably should be grateful for the threats. Imagine if they killed me and my children heard the news on the radio.

I left everything, gave up all I had, and went to Medellín. We had only just enough money for the tickets and found our way to a friend's house. When she saw how many we were, though—I had my son and my friend's children with me—she said she could only put us up for a day or two until we found somewhere else to go.

Well, I found some clothes to wash and started making a little something each day. We didn't have much, but it was enough for all of us to eat. I walked to work and back, so I could use the bus fare to buy the chance. The lady where we stayed was hard on us, especially on my friend's daughter and me, and I got religious. I'd cry and pray, pray and cry, but couldn't seem to get lucky anywhere. Then one Friday I sent the boy out to buy a ticket— there goes another five hundred pesos, I thought—and he came back yelling: "Mama, Mama, we hit the number last night!"

"What do you mean? Oh my blessed Lord, what have you done for this Negra?"

I ran back to the lottery stand with my friend and the man told us we had won 224 thousand pesos with our number. Our blessed 255! Oh, my God! I thanked Him for not abandoning me after all the bad things they'd done to me. I thanked all the souls in purgatory—they're the ones who protect the working people—and to show my thanks, I decided to do something for my friend. She'd been good to me, giving me money for the children and taking me into her house and helping us when we needed it. Finally, I could do something for her!

Early next morning, I took her shopping and spent sixty thousand pesos on things she needed! I got her everything— glasses, cutlery, and plates, a heavy blanket for the cold, a real suitcase so she wouldn't have to use shopping bags when she moved around, and a corn remover because she suffers a lot from

corns. Then I took her to the beauty salon, and she had a permanent. I bought a few things as well and fixed myself up and put on
a nice dress and shoes and, on Sunday, went to the bus station and
took a bus to Bogotá, where my children were waiting for me.

When I got on that bus I had no idea what was waiting for me
here. I was worried that if my children weren't there I wouldn't
know where to go. But when I arrived at about four in the afternoon, there they were! I was so happy seeing them again, hugging
them and seeing they were all right. I told them to get a taxi.

"What do you mean, a taxi?" they asked.

"That's what I said. A taxi. I've ridden on enough buses
today. I want to arrive in style!"

But when we arrived at the house, my bubble burst. The
husband of the lady of the house was also in jail, and there were
twelve people living there, all crammed in like rabbits in a hutch.
When I saw that, I shook off my exhaustion and turned right
around and went off to buy a cot we could all take turns sleeping
on. I gave what was left over to the lady to help with expenses.

I can't seem to find myself here in Bogotá. When you're used
to the country and the chickens and roosters, it's very hard to get
used to living all together in one room. And, poor as the barrios
in Apartadó are, there's not nearly as much garbage and dirt
around, or stench outside, as there is here.

I have nothing bad to say about people from the countryside
and towns like Apartadó because they've suffered an awful lot
and bled a great deal. But there are some envious people here
who think as the rich do: everything a poor person has is stolen.
They say things that hurt you. I started selling *arepas* here on the
street close to a school, for example, and a little in front of me
were some more people from Urabá doing the same thing. One

day, some girls from one of the schools here looked at us and said, "You're turning this into a barrio of displaced people."

Well, when I heard that I wanted to tell those girls what it's like where I am from and tell them why we came here and about all the crimes that were committed against us. But what could I do? Nothing but swallow my pride, and say nothing. That's how silence humiliates you. Another time, we were asleep one night when some shots in the street outside the house woke us up. The state we were all in after fleeing our home, imagine, we thought the paras had come for us! With the shots, we heard a voice, "Come out of there, you displaced sons-of-bitches, fucking guerrillas! Come out and die!"

It turned out to be one of the neighbors who'd had too much to drink and decided to make fun of us for being displaced. It was a joke. But jokes have their poison and drunks say what they really feel. Things here are difficult.

To get by in Bogotá, I've had to learn to control the expressions on my face, because when you're not used to something here, it makes you feel ashamed. I've had to get used to a lot of things here. Going to the nuns and telling them I don't have anything in the house, for example, or telling them more personal things, like when it's two in the afternoon, and my family hasn't had anything to eat yet. God bless the nuns at Fe y Alegría who've been so kind to us. You have to get used to that kind of situation here because if you don't, you'll die of hunger.

That's how things were when Blanca arrived in November 1997. The truth is I hadn't had any real peace of mind without her. You've got to have the people you love around you, especially in the kind of times we're living in, and I'd thought a lot about Blanca, her husband, and my grandchildren. I'd called her and asked her to come to Bogotá, knowing that we'd all worry a lot less if we were together. Things were worse than ever there, and they were after her, figuring that would be the only way we'd all go back to Apartadó again. And the truth is, if they had killed her, I couldn't have stood it here and would have gone back to her funeral.

Blanca brought her two children with her, but her husband stayed behind. He ended up having to get out of there too, though, because of what the paracos did to the couple who lived in front of his house. It was terrible. They killed the lady—she was my daughter's godmother—and her husband. Blanca's husband is a determined and strong man and has never been a coward. But what they did made him dirty his pants. It's not his fault, everybody reacts differently to fear like that. The killers walked across the street and waited there, and, when everyone thought the killing was over, a lady went over to help with the bodies, and they shot her, too.

When Blanca came to Bogotá, she wasn't planning to stay for good. She wanted to see how things were first. She didn't want to leave Apartadó because her husband had a good job on one of the bananeras. But my pleading as her mother and my tears ended up convincing her to stay, and all four families— fifteen adults and two small children—moved into two rooms together. We all slept on the floor. It was only five meters by two, and we all had to fit in there somehow. You'd see a row of heads from the door right over to the wall and, after we'd all gone to bed, no one could move or the whole thing would "come apart." Only the ones by the door could get up to go to the bathroom. The good thing about it was the heat of all those bodies; the bad thing was the lack of air. We'd wake up all sweaty, feeling suffo-

cated. But we were all alive and together, and I was happy for
that. My only complaint were the fleas. We fumigated the house,
the blankets, everything, but they were everywhere. Where I
come from, only dogs have fleas. How they've enjoyed all the
fresh meat we brought them!

We all had to tighten our belts to pay the rent and buy food.
We paid fifty thousand pesos in rent and spent ten thousand on
food. We'd buy giblets and bones mostly, so we'd have enough
for the rent. It meant a lot of work. Thank God, all of us women
got along well so if one got a kilo of rice and another some panela,
well, that's what we'd eat. If we only had enough for rice, we'd
eat rice. Or if we had enough to get a pound of bones, we'd
make a soup for everybody. No one was ever told they couldn't
eat because they hadn't contributed. No, sir! The displaced help
one another because we all know what we've been through in
this life. We've all suffered more than enough.

Like Nubia, La Catira, for example. The first time we saw
her was here in the barrio. She had her young son with her, and
she was pregnant. She'd fled Villavicencio and come here to
Bogotá. Before that, she and her husband and kids had fled
somewhere else and gone to Villavicencio. She showed up here
the same day they killed her husband. She got a ride in a truck
outside the cemetery there and drove right on to Bogotá. The
truck driver felt sorry for her and her kids and bought them
lunch on the way. Well, she arrived with a hundred pesos in her
pocket. My daughters saw her wandering around by herself,
looking sick because of the pregnancy and took her to the hospital in Kennedy. She had her baby by caesarian section, and they
gave her a bill for eight hundred thousand pesos. Where could
she ever get that much money?

The doctor said if she didn't have it, she could start begging in the halls there in hospital, just after her operation. She could only come up with three thousand pesos. By begging in the street and some other odd jobs, we all came up with another fifty thousand for her. Well, La Catira arranged to sell her baby to a nurse at the hospital but the nuns here wouldn't let her and went to see the doctor on her behalf. We settled the hospital bill with what we had, and she and her two children came to live here with us.

There are eighteen of us now, and it's a squeeze but you do what you can. La Catira earns a little something making conjugal visits to a man in jail. She met him when she went with one of her friends to visit her husband, who's in jail because of La Chinita. She's able to buy some food with what she makes. I don't agree with what she's doing, but who am I to say what you can or can't do when your stomach is empty?

My last visit to Apartadó saddened me more than I can say. It was so hard to leave, knowing that this time it was for good! That all I'd spent on the house and all the work I'd put into it over the years was for nothing. Because whenever it needed to be painted, I did it; if it needed cement or plastering, I took care of it…. I looked at the walls, I got down and felt the floors, and poured some water on my plants for the last time. I went into every room and sat down on the beds…. I wanted to put all of it in my head somehow and take it away with me. I stopped in front of a mirror and stared at my reflection.

"Goodbye, Osiris," I said. Then I walked out, leaving all my dreams there once and for all.

I know why they're after me. It started when that captain found out I knew who killed my son. I'll say it again here and now: they were the ones who killed him because they told me who gave the order and which killers did the job. They know it, I know it, and God knows it, and the proof of that is that a little while after it happened, the captain and his killers were all transferred out of there.

What I don't know, though, is why they want to kill everybody like that. There's a story they used to tell in the barrio—I don't know if it's true or not—about Policarpa being on top of a whole lot of oil, with all the people living on top of the wealth. They say they discovered oil when a black, sticky mud came out of some cracks in the ground during the big earthquake in Urabá. I remember seeing the black mud, but I didn't think anything of it at the time. After that, they say, some foreigners arrived—I don't know which country they were from—because people from outside the country were interested in the oil. Since then, they've been told to get rid of the people, of all of us, because we're in the way.

Maybe it would be better for us if we didn't talk about what happened, about our history. But if we don't tell people about it, all of our dead will remain dead forever. We may have to bury them, but that doesn't mean we are ever going to forget them. At night here, when I'm trying to get used to the cold and the sad situation we are all in, I comfort myself by thinking back to some of the good times I had in Apartadó. I had a lot of things in my house: a dresser, a television, a rocking chair, a couple of pictures, and even a print of the *Sagrado Corazón*, the Sacred Heart. And before leaving Apartadó, I'd always find a way to sneak back into Policarpa and have a look at my things. I didn't live there anymore, but they were still my things, and I wanted to make sure they were all still there. I'd sweep and mop and put everything in its place and then go back downtown to where I was living. I remember at night, I'd sit outside on a bench on the

patio listening to music and looking up at the stars in the dark
sky. I had some chairs there, they weren't expensive ones or anything, but at least anyone who wanted could sit down with you
there and cool off. You could feel the peace.

I've lost track of what's going on in Apartadó now because I
don't have the three thousand pesos it costs to call. I just know that
some people moved into my house and are living there. I don't
know who they are. I worked for everything I had there. Worked
like a man in the hills and like a woman at home. I've never
shied away from anything, and, if it comes to that again here, I'll
do the same. You can never say you won't do something because
you might find out later you have no choice in the matter. But I
won't go back there! I won't go back to a place where no one dies
of sickness anymore. When you can call, they never tell you so
and so got sick and died, only that someone killed him. Over
time here, we've all started to relax a little, but the women who
go to visit at *La Picota* * said they were told we're all on a video
they have and sooner or later they're going to come after us. I
won't run anymore! I've had enough. All I can do now is wait
and see if they really do find us here. We are in God's hands now.

---

* High security jail in Bogotá.

Chapter 8

Nubia, La Catira

I

I grew up on the plains of San Juan, a huge swath of flat land that seemed to have no end to it. For as far as you looked in any direction, there was only land. We were like curious deer growing up, always looking off into the distance trying to guess whether the person coming was a stranger or someone we knew. You'd see them first as black specks coming out of the tall grass, growing bigger and bigger as they came closer, until we could make out who they were. Then we'd put on the *tinto* to offer whoever it was. Or we'd hide. You learned to watch who you were with out there by yourself and to pay close attention to what visitors said.

My father worked as a hand on different ranches until we were grown, and we never knew him well. He'd show up, talk to my mother, leave her some money, and off he'd go again. It was always like that. Until the day she told us she wanted to settle down somewhere else, so we'd have some land and wouldn't have to always be on the move. She got a small piece of land at the foot of a hill in the Costa Rica hamlet, fenced off a lot, and put up a store. With what little money that gave her, she began to clear land slowly and learned how to plant coffee. Everyone there was a farmer—most were from Tolima—and they were all hard workers. The houses would all fill up with coffee at harvest time, and everyone lived off what it earned them.

But prosperity breeds envy and envy brings evil, and before long thieves showed up, men who, instead of working like everyone else, held people up and robbed them. They used to stop the mule trains and steal the coffee or ambush the coffee pickers on their way home with their wages and take their money. The bandits were from a place called Angosturas del Guape. They were almost like a family, *Los Trifones*. They were armed, knew the land well, and had people working for them. Los Trifones had been robbing and killing since *La Violencia*, and everybody had heard of them.

They say that's why the guerrillas showed up. Some say they came over from Medellín del Ariari or Mesetas; others, that they had their camp by the headwaters of the Duda River in the Rincón de los Varela, over towards Cundinamarca. Anyway, they went after Los Trifones and cleaned them up lock, stock, and barrel.

They killed an awful lot of bandits with a shot in the neck or a bullet in the forehead, and the robberies stopped. The campesinos, well sure, they were grateful because that was defending their livelihood.

After that, the guerrillas began to take over. As a girl, I saw them before I saw policemen. I remember one day in Granada my mother hit me in the mouth after I asked her why the "muchachos" had such nice haircuts. We were standing beside some soldiers at the time, and their uniforms didn't mean anything to me.

The guerrillas were good people, not rude or bad-mannered. Sometimes they'd stop by the house and chat or teach the kids songs: "Long live Viotá the Red, long live the Revolution …" was one we all knew without having any idea where Viotá was or what a revolution was. The guerrillas taught me to read and write, and I always wanted them to take me to their camp. But my mother didn't like me talking to them. She said they were men of war, and we shouldn't have anything to do with them. But we did.

My mother had a reputation as a hard worker because she'd built the farm by herself without the help of any man. Before long, the store she opened was supplying all the hamlets in the area, and she was appointed town counselor in San Juan. She was well known and respected by everyone. I remember her working day and night to get the bulldozer that finally opened up the road to Cunimía, the zinc tiles for the school in Badó Hondo, and medicine for the health clinic in Buenos Aires. She became involved in so many things that she didn't have time for the store. She was also named president of the Unión Patriótica when everybody around here thought the guerrillas were going to become more involved in that and even turn over the weapons to the government.

But the more popular my mother got, the worse the store did. She let everybody buy on credit and that turned out to be why she was killed. It was the ones who owed her the most who went to the army and accused her of selling to the guerrillas. My mother helped everybody, and, when we looked at her ledger after she died, all we saw were debts and more debts and the names of campesinos from all over the hamlets who owed her money.

One day, she left for Granada to buy some grain, pay the Bavaria beer distributor, and make a complaint against a couple of men who refused to pay her some money they'd owed for a long time. She left early, so she'd be back early. The only thing that got back early, though, was the news she'd been killed. I was fourteen, and my brothers were older, already men, and we ran outside together to see what had happened. All we found was the blood beside the Ariari River. She used to cross over there at La Playa instead of going down to Puerto de los Perros or Puerto Caldas. The water was high and running fast and they threw her body in.

The current washed her up under the Guillermo León Valencia Bridge three days later, and we buried her in San Juan. People came from all over the *llanos*: Senator Pedro Nel Jiménez, from Villavicencio, a representative from the Camara, Octavio Vargas, and the UP mayors of Lejanías, Mesetas, and San Juan. It was a beautiful and very moving ceremony. My brothers got drunk and swore they'd avenge her death and, since then, they've continued to drink a lot and have become very aggressive and rude.

They killed Pedro exactly a year after my mother's death, as if to celebrate our pain. He was taking the mules along. There were five of them loaded with coffee up ahead of him on the path with the *arriero*, the mule driver, and five more behind him.

They say the arriero sensed something was wrong and tried to go back and warn Pedro, but they got him and killed him with machetes, so there'd be no shots to hear. They killed Pedro the same way. There must have been a lot of them because Pedro was big and could fight. His thick wrists and heavy fists had earned him the respect of everyone around the plaza in San Juan. They whacked at him until the machete bent. He was mostly in pieces by then, his head hanging off his neck, and the killers left him that way. But he was still alive and a neighbor was with him in his last moments. He asked her to move his head out of the puddle it was in and to clean him up as well as she could. Before he died, he told her: "Look, Doña Clotilde, they were soldiers from the Vargas battalion, under the command of Captain Turriago. The same ones who killed my mother."

We buried him beside my mother in San Juan.

A few days later, my father showed. I didn't even recognize him. He said, "We're going to sell what we can and go to San José de Fragua, in Caquetá. It's time to get you away from all this bloodshed."

He was right. A little while before we left, they killed Doña Clotilde, our neighbor. They were afraid she'd say something to someone and tortured her horribly. She screamed, "Kill me! Please kill me! But stop torturing me!"

No one ever found her body. They say the army has cemeteries in their barracks. They wanted to know everything she'd told people before she died to make sure her secret died with her.

Well, we left the farm, the store, the house, and everything else. My brothers moved off their land, and we haven't seen them since. When there's so much suffering and pain, sometimes you just don't want to hear anymore about it. A few days after we left, the guerrillas came down and killed fifteen soldiers along the Guéjar River. By then, though, we were on our way, and it was almost a year later before we heard the news.

II

The town of San José de Fragua was built on the shore of the Fraguachorroso River. It is a torrent of a river with treacherous currents, and the town grew because of that treachery. Mule drivers arriving there with their loads of wood and corn had to wait three, four, even five days before they could get across it. People started selling things and putting up hotels and places to stay, and, finally, they built houses there. Before long, there was a school, and the Protestants had built their temple.

I won't lie and say it was anything else but coca that kept us going once we got off the bus in San José. There was nothing else to do there. Coca saved us, and we are grateful for that. A friend of my father offered him a piece of land to grow coca on and sell back to her at the price she set. My father became a day laborer, and our food and whatever else we needed was subtracted from his wages. He made just enough that way to make it worth his while to continue. Plus a little extra for us to clear our own patch of land.

I started working for the nuns, running errands and washing their clothes. They helped us a great deal. We lived that way for two years until my father got tired of working the land. He'd always liked to have cattle and horses, so he bought a pair of mules and went into the hills to take gasoline from place to place. Coca made him the money to get started. During one of his trips to Belén de los Andaquíes, on the high path by the headwaters of the river, one of his mules stepped in a bog. As my father was trying to pull him out, the animal kicked his leg and and broke it.

Hardly anyone travels on that path, and there was no one to help him. It took him two days to hobble to Belén, and, by then, the bone had split into pieces. It didn't heal well and even though he stayed in a hammock for the better part of six months, the leg never worked well again. He had to get used to working sitting down.

Well, like all *llaneros*, he knew how to make sandals, so he set up a little shop to make them out of leather and tire rubber. But no one in the mountains uses sandals, and he couldn't make a go of it. So he tried his luck at mending rubber boots. Rubber is difficult to work with because it melts when it's heated and splits open when it cools down. But he was patient and persistent and learned the secret, and before you knew it, he'd become San José's shoemaker. Some people took him their leather shoes, but his specialty was rubber boots, and there were none better than his. Whenever there was a lull in the coca business and the price dropped, he'd make good money because everyone wanted to patch up their old boots instead of throwing them away and buying new ones.

We lived a good life for a couple of years in La Fragua, and, during that time, I fell in love with Elver. He'd been chosen to be teacher of the new school by the parents' association, but the government never paid him, and the kids were always working in the coca fields instead of going to school, so he gave up teaching and became the jeep driver on the run to Belén. Elver was a good boy and a good worker. Neither of us was in any hurry to get married. When he had the early morning run, he'd sleep in town, and I'd stay with him. Other times, I'd wait for him to come and visit. Elver got along with everybody and didn't have any enemies.

The guerrillas ran things, and no one argued with them. As

long as you didn't fight and got along with your neighbors and weren't a thief, a drunk, or drug user, they treated you well. The only complaint you did hear were mothers saying the commanders were trying to force their children to join them. No mother wants that to happen, although there were some cases of "wayward" kids being straightened out after going with the guerrillas. Kids can earn a lot if they work hard in the coca fields, and that brings bad habits and poor judgment. A lot of kids started going bad quickly, and their own parents sent them off to the guerrillas to straighten them out. And they did. They shaped up, but by then, they didn't want to leave the guerrillas.

The girls liked the guerrillas because of how imposing they looked in their uniforms. And because people paid attention to them and did what they said, the younger ones matured quickly. Of course there are exceptions. I knew one boy who ended up being executed by the guerrillas because they couldn't get him to stop using *basuco*. He sniffed all the time. He was an orphan, and I am sure he missed his parents. But they warned him several times, and after that, well, there's no appeal.

And there's also a problem with the girls. A lot of them decide to join the guerrillas to get away from the routine at home and because in the hills they're free to pair off with anyone they want, as long as everybody knows about it. There's always the chance they'll get pregnant, though, and you can't fight or even cook for the other guerrillas once your stomach starts growing. The commanders make them take birth control pills. But some forget, especially since they're not used to taking them, and become pregnant. A lot of girls leave the guerrillas to have their babies, then leave the babies with their mothers, sisters, or aunts.

I remember one who came down to have her baby, but then

didn't want to leave it with anyone. She tried to take off with the baby and the guerrillas caught her. She'd been a radio operator, and that's an important job because you have a lot of information. You know the codes, the places the guerrillas are camped, and what they're planning. Well, trying to take off like that was her death sentence. Not even the fact she had a little baby changed their minds, and they treated her as a deserter and shot her. We all felt terrible, and people complained, but it didn't matter. The guerrillas just went on about their business, living their way according to their laws, and things started to go bad.

My father and I set up a little store, and sometimes we'd talk to the guerrillas when they came in to drink a pop or buy cigarettes. One night, I guess it was about eight o'clock, two of them came in and told us they were deserting. Neither had seen his family in years, and they'd been denied permission to visit them. They told us they'd had enough of that life. I remember one of them was dark-skinned and from Roldanillo. They didn't have any money, so we gave them some pop and bread, and they asked us not to say we'd seen them if anybody asked.

A couple of days went by and no one else came down from the hills. People said the soldiers had gone up and that the guerrillas were getting ready for them. Then we saw the two that had deserted coming up. This time, though, they were dressed in army uniforms and were leading a group of soldiers. I suppose they'd tired of running and had gone to a cheap hotel in Sabaneta to rest. Someone told the army, though, and they caught them. They beat them, tied them up, and took them away. They had them a couple of days until they agreed to guide the soldiers up through the hills in exchange for their lives.

And that's what they did. The soldiers walked through town,

slowly, taking everything in, and then left, taking the two deserters with them. Everything was quiet after that for a while and there was a calm in town. People went on about their lives, working the coca, and struggling to make ends meet. The guerrillas came by from time to time, getting everybody together for something or other. During one of their meetings, they told us the paramilitaries were on their way. They told us to be on guard with our eyes open, that we'd be the ones to suffer, and, above all, that no one should talk to strangers or people they didn't know.

Time passed. The guerrillas stopped taxing the coca farmers as they'd been doing and started making the man who bought from them pay the tax instead. He used to pick up the "merchandise" in Don Anselmo's store. Don Anselmo would cheat you given half the chance, and he was the one the farmers paid. He charged each farmer less for their "merca" than he sold it for, and the guerrillas took the difference. But Anselmo was always looking to make money, so he began paying the farmers less and pocketing the difference. The farmers told the guerrilla commander, but Anselmo was too crafty and shrewd for them, and the commander didn't believe them.

Rumors that the paramilitaries were coming continued, and people started getting very nervous. Anyone who'd collaborated in one way or another with the guerrillas began thinking about leaving. That was a lot of people, because the guerrillas organized everything in that town: a bazaar to raise money for a road, a beauty pageant for a bridge, or a *tejo* tournament to clear a road. When the town's water tank was swept away by the river, it was the community junta that organized people to build another one. There were festivals, and everybody helped out by donating money, a pig to roast, some chickens to eat, or helped making the *sancocho*. Some did more than others, but everybody did something. That was how the town got its water supply back. But the junta did what the guerrillas told them to do. Everybody knew that. So when people began saying the paras were coming, those who'd collaborated the most and were the wealthiest left town. The rest of us stayed put. We had no money to leave with and nowhere to go.

Well, the day finally arrived and the paras came into town. They arrived at midday. The first ones we saw were the same two deserters we'd seen guiding the army. They had a hooded man with them, someone we'd never seen before. Or so we thought. The paras had a megaphone and ordered everyone into the plaza. No one wanted to go. Everybody was scared of what was going to happen. And they were right. The hooded man started pointing to people: this one, yes; that one, no; that one, yes; on and on like that. When he finished, he said there were four or five missing and the paras sent a handful of their killers to their houses to get them. They only found two of them. They tied them to a post there in the plaza and shot them. They accused my father of being the guerrilla's shoemaker and shot him right away. The army thinks anyone who wears rubber boots is a guerrilla or a friend of the guerrillas. They also killed the owner of the drugstore, saying he was the one selling birth control pills to the guerrilleras. None of our screams or pleas stopped the killing.

Between the shots, there was absolute silence in the plaza. So absolute I am sure you could hear it miles away. No one even cried there in the plaza, watching that evil and feeling it deep inside us. Each one of our lives depended on the hooded man and whether or not he pointed to us. But the man was missing a finger on the hand he used and soon everyone knew it was Don Anselmo.

They shot another five there in the plaza. Then they filled their truck with another group they wanted to make talk before killing. The road out of town was littered with body parts. They used a chainsaw on them. The only ones who were saved were Don Anselmo's friends and the ones with money who left town before the paras arrived. The army arrived after we had finished praying for the dead.

Elver took my hand and led me to his father's house. The old man was a *valluno* from the town of Tuluá. I was still crying for my father as we packed, and the three of us left San José. We drove through Belén and on to Florencia and slept there. My father-in-law didn't say a word during the whole trip. It was all very difficult for him because it was the second time he'd been forced to leave like that. It was my second time, too, but I was twenty-four and he was over eighty.

The old man had lived two full lives, one before leaving Tuluá and the other in Caquetá. On the drive north from Florencia, he began to talk about how he arrived years earlier, where he'd stopped and where he'd slept. It was as if he were reliving the past again as we went. He had walked from Tuluá to Cali and from Cali to Popayán. From Popayán, he'd gone over the mountains to Neiva. As we drove along, it was like he was saying goodbye to all those roads and journeys of his past. He was downcast and depressed the whole way, saying he felt like he'd wasted his life, swimming around in circles in water he could never get out of. The trip back was too much for him and by the time we got to Cali, he was dead. We drove to Tuluá and buried him. My father's death was terrible, but my father-in-law's death made me very sad. In my mind, I saw myself there in the same water, paddling away without knowing if I was going forward or backwards.

In Tuluá, we went to the office of the Red de Solidaridad* to see if they could help us. They gave us forms and more forms to fill out and sent us all over the place. Then they told us we needed recommendations from some well-known and well-established people, people whose conduct was "beyond reproach." We didn't know what to do because no one knew us in that town. My father-in-law's brother had a daughter living in Tuluá, and that's where we ended up. She told us there was a priest who gave recommendations in exchange for donations he said were for building a church in the barrio. And there was a well-placed Liberal politician who sold recommendations. You had to take cash to both of them.

Well, we did that and got a letter of recommendation from each of them. Those two must be making a fortune off all the displaced people that have come down from hamlets in the mountains like La Aurora, Puerto Frazadas, and Monte Loro. And it must be a business others are involved in, because in the camps for the displaced that the mayor's office set up, there were rumors the paras were planning to come and kill everyone they'd missed in the hills. People were tripping over one another running to get those recommendations. When we had ours, a man from the Red told us they were setting up a displaced community in the Guachaca in the Sierra Nevada de Santa Marta. We were thinking of trying that until a fellow who was in line with us said, "That's one of Hernán Giraldo's programs. He's the one responsible for the worst massacres on the Atlantic coast: La Honduras, La Negra,

---

* The government organization responsible for attending to the needs of Colombia's most vulnerable populations.

Mejor Esquina. He's trying to get people in there and buy their loyalty, so he won't lose the area to the guerrillas or to his sworn enemy, Adán Rojas.*"

We didn't need to hear any more about it. We didn't want to go from a bad situation to something worse, so we went to Villavicencio, and from there to Puerto Rico, Meta, where I had some relatives.

III

The town of Puerto Rico was made for Elver and me. He was born in the jungle, and there it was, and I had the plains. The town is on the Ariari River, with the mouth of the Guéjar and Cuminía Rivers in front of it and the plains of La Virgen and Pororio spread out behind it. I had known Father Elvira, the town's Spanish priest, when I was a girl, and, although he was no longer there, people helped us find a place and settle in.

Elver and I decided to work together. He agreed to use the money from the car to buy cattle, and, since I'd grown up around cattle, I began to run the business. We rented a small house on the edge of the plain with a view of the Candelaria Ranch, pure grassland. That's where we pastured our thirty head, all two-year-olds I bought in San Martín in spite of my fears of going there because it was full of paramilitaries like all the other ranching towns. Elver was always a hard worker, and to keep from becoming bored, he got hired on as a substitute teacher at the school. No one had anything bad to say about us, and we kept to ourselves. We were happy, and I got pregnant and had my first child a year after we arrived.

---

* Hernán Giraldo and Adán Rojas are United Self-Defense Forces of Colombia (AUC) paramilitary commanders. Rojas was captured in 2000.

The coca from Guaviare and the crops that grew in the Guéjar and Cuminía mountains all made their way through Puerto Rico, and the constant hustle and bustle and noise of trucks and buses made it difficult to sleep. I was always nervous about so much coming and going, but, busy as we were with the cattle and Elver with his classes, we kept to ourselves and had no time to get into any trouble. Or at least that's what we thought.

We worked that way until we sold our first lot of cattle and doubled the money we'd started with. We'd see the guerrillas every now and again but never paid them anything, in spite of the fact they knew how many head of cattle we had. I suppose they were just fattening up the pot. Time passed, the cattle grew well, and we were content. I think I became pregnant again during that time.

Then the guerrillas attacked the town. We hadn't heard any rumors, and no one expected it. It was towards evening, and the town's electric generator had been turned off for the night. I was changing my baby's diaper before putting him down for the night when the shouts began in the street: "Everybody out! Out now! There's going to be an attack. Everybody as you are, hurry, to the cemetery! You'll be safe there. As long as you do as you're told, you'll be fine."

It was a guerrillera, a woman, with a megaphone. I grabbed hold of my baby and said a prayer to María Auxiliadora. Then I said to him, "We'll run to Don Ricardo's. The others have already gone and we won't catch up."

Don Ricardo was a cattle buyer who was always very fond of Elver and me. But when we got to his house and knocked on the door, no one opened it. We pounded and pounded but, even though we heard people inside, no one opened the door, and we had no choice but to head for the cemetery. The shooting had already begun, and, as we ran, and I had to jump over guerrillas lying on the ground with their guns ready.

The cemetery was full when we got there with people hiding behind all the headstones. The expensive ones were the best because they were taller and built of cement. For the first time in my life, I was more afraid of the living than of the dead; it was almost better to be their friend because at least they could protect you.

We could hear the shooting in the plaza and the port—not only the noise from the guns and the mortars, but the flashes of light from the fires they'd started and from bullets that were slicing through the sky from side to side. The ground shook every time one of the bombs exploded against the police station. It was like hell. The strangest thing of all was that in the cemetery, we were all so scared that no one was even breathing loudly. You could hear a pin drop, it was so quiet.

The explosions went on and on. Guerrillas kept pouring into town, jumping out of barges they'd made on the river and trucks that were driving in behind the town from the plains. They had the police in the middle. The police weren't prepared, but they were fierce and brave and fought like tigers with their backs to the wall. They had huge tunnels they'd dug and some other cement structures that looked like pears with holes in the front where they'd stick their guns out and fire. They kept the lights on there all night because they were afraid. But in the dark, it was the light that became their enemy. Whenever the police went into town, they'd be afraid. And they'd watch each other's back when one went to make a phone call or drink a pop with a girl.

Then, suddenly, it was quiet. The only sound was an army plane circling high above. Well, that was even worse because then the real war began. It started machine-gunning and dropping bombs where they thought the guerrillas were hiding. But they were just guessing, because the bombs fell all over the place. We felt the bursts of gunfire, the taque-taque-taque and the red flashes lighting up our faces as we lay hiding there under the dead. The truth is they fired at everything, at the town and at the houses. It didn't matter if there were women and children there, they fired wherever they thought there were guerrillas. That's where the bombs exploded.

It was that plane that hurt the guerrillas the most and did the most damage to the town. The government did the most damage with its airplane. I looked around me at all those bullets flying and asked myself how long I had until one of them hit me. Then I thought about the children and old people. Oh God, I thought, what if they kill us and just the children and old people are left? And as if to make everything even worse, none of us had any money or any way to get away.

With the dawn's light, the calm returned. We walked out of the cemetery slowly to look around at what was left. People started bringing out their pots and organizing a sancocho, and we were eating that when all of a sudden, the bullets started flying again and the gas cylinders exploded against the wall of the police station. Then the plane was back. An awful lot of guerrillas took part in that attack. And not just from the 44 Front, the ones that operate in the area, but from Sumapaz, El Retorno, and from Vichada as well. Strangers who didn't know the lay of the land. We heard them asking where the river or the bank was or where the doctor lived. They didn't know where they were. I don't think the ones in the plane did either. They almost blew up the police station. There was an explosion inside it after one of their passes. We never knew if it was a bomb from the plane or the guerrillas. But the police weren't giving in and kept returning fire.

Then all of a sudden the ground began to shake again. This time it wasn't from an explosion but from something big that was approaching. Everything shook so much we thought the houses were going to come down. No one expected what we saw next: an armoured tank driving off a barge on the river. Well, they drove it to the police station and then used it as a bulldozer to knock down the walls. Guerrillas swarmed inside. There was nothing the police could do, short on ammunition, almost out of water, and overrun like that. There were usually about fifty of them inside. Many of them lived with their wives and some with their children, but that night there were only thirty-three. The guerrillas killed five of them and took the other twenty-eight prisoners.

We found out later the guerrillas attacked Puerto Lleras that same night. The army arrived later that same Saturday though. The army didn't get to Puerto Rico until Monday, and who knows where the policemen they took away with them were by then. All we've heard about them since are the messages their mothers send them on the radio, La Voz del Llano.*

As soon as they filed them out of the police station with their hands on their heads and left town, people rushed in there like vultures after a kill to steal whatever they could find—clothes, shoes, radios, flashlights. It was townspeople, not the guerrillas, who did that.

---

* "The Voice of the Plains," a national radio station based in Meta.

The attack started at about five on Friday afternoon, July 10, and ended on Monday morning when the army arrived. Sixty hours of shooting and fear, not counting the time we made the sancocho. The government won the battle because the guerrillas don't have any planes. There were a lot of guerrillas killed. Many, many killed. At least forty of the two hundred that attacked the town. We saw a lot of guerrilleras afterwards crying and saying they had never come out of an attack in such bad shape before. It was the first combat for almost all of them. They were youngsters, and they didn't know where they were.

The army stayed in town for a week and then left. Then the guerrillas came back, got everyone together in front of the rubble that had been the police station and told us, "The paramilitaries are on their way. Anyone who wants to stay here will have to deal with them. Those who want to leave had better get going. We can only defend those who defend themselves. In other words, those who get a gun and come with us."

Some of the young ones went with them, but most didn't. And most of the ones that stayed, like us, moved on to Villavicencio.

We ended up in La Reliquia barrio, one of those land invasions that people call Malvinas.* It's a piece of land with more than thirty-five hundred families on it. That's about twenty thousand people. We settled in the best we could and started to think of ways to get back on our feet again. I figured we could sell the cattle

---

* A "land invasion" occurs when the landless and/or homeless occupy a piece of land and set up a community or neighborhood, often provoking violent clashes with the government, landowners, or paramilitaries.

The ironic nickname of "Malvinas" refers to the Islas Malvinas, the Spanish name of the Falkland Islands—the British colony that Argentina occupied in 1982, provoking a bloody war with Britain.

and do something with the money. But when times are bad, it's hard to sell anything for a reasonable price. All the prices fall.

Elver got a job teaching in the school built by the Comité de Impulso de la Asamblea del Meta. The mayor of Villavicencio promised to legalize the land we were living on, but the owners were against it and threatened us. The politicians had to deal with the problem of so many families living crammed together in those conditions with no work. The landowners and the mayor continued to fight over that until the paramilitaries arrived in the barrio.

They shot Elver five times and killed him in the school. He'd never been afraid to speak his mind and had become something of a leader. I was just getting off the bus from Puerto Rico when I heard the news. They took Elver to the hospital to die, and they gave me his body after finishing the autopsy. I didn't know what to do. Whether to run away, to cry, or to scream. Thank God I had the boy with me, because otherwise I don't think I would have had the will to go on. On top of that, I was feeling the nausea of another pregnancy.

I didn't want to go home after that. So after the funeral, I came here to Bogotá to find a refuge. Every day, more and more people who have been beaten down and defeated are coming here, people who've been forced out of the barrios they've set up in Villavicencio, Granada, and Acacías because the paramilitaries are there as well. I was too scared to go back to Puerto Rico to sell the cattle, afraid my boy would end up an orphan. That money was lost. I ended up adrift, at the mercy of the current, and the current brought me here to Bogotá to have my baby. The nurse who took care of me in the hospital offered to buy my baby for a couple from France who wanted one. I decided to do it but had to say no at the last minute when people from the barrio said they wouldn't let me. Now, I live like a broody hen without a nest, moving from place to place. A prisoner in La Picota who used to buy and sell coca and who I met in La Fragua fell in love with me and is giving me money for me and my children while I decide what to do with the rest of my life.

APPENDIX

"Desterrados"

Forced Displacement in Colombia*

Mabel González Bustelo

Translated by Allison M. Rohe

Displacements in Colombia cannot be analyzed as a consequence or a collateral effect of actions perpetrated by armed actors. They are not an "effect" of the conflict; rather they are a weapon of war and part of a strategy to accumulate economic gains. Displacements tend to take place in areas rich in natural resources, plagued by political violence and fighting, where violence is used as a tool to control the land. However, the underlying motives are even more profound and often hidden.[1]

Displacements often take place in different contexts that occur simultaneously: human rights violations, armed conflicts, social conflicts (such as workers' demands), land reforms, implementation of mega-projects, fights for (or against) illicit crops. The

* This is an edited excerpt from a longer report by the same title. The report is available for download from Haymarket Books at http://www.haymarketbooks.org. Mabel González Bustelo is a journalist and researcher for the Peace Research Center (Centro de Investigación para la Paz, CIP-FUHEM), in Madrid. The initial version of this document was prepared after the author carried out a field study in Colombia from June to October 2001. The Web site of the CIP is http://www.fuhem.es/cip. The author's e-mail address is mabelgonzalez@teleline.es.

causes are not only the actors themselves, but also the social, economic, and political factors at the root of these historically unresolved conflicts. As such, displacements are linked to historic tensions and contradictions, such as

- large urban migrations that have not been accompanied by an industrialization process (revolution) or economic development to ensure that this new labor force is absorbed into the formal sector

- permanent rural colonization that has never been regulated by the state, resulting in coexistence that is organized by the local people and groups rather than the state

- absence of state institutions in large regions and semi-feudal regional and local structures used to wield power

- increased cooperation among the armed actors, who have turned violence into a means to serve their interests and to guarantee their survival

Historically, land occupancy based on private appropriation has been driven by an orientation on foreign markets (as evidenced in the cycles undergone by such products as quinine, indigo, tobacco, livestock, coffee, ivory palm, rubber, oil, and illicit crops), boosting the expansion of farmland borders. Land tenure has followed a pattern based on individually or family-owned properties maintained through violent means, and the occupation of the best lands. The displaced populations that came from bordering farmland areas settled on the remaining land, considered unsuitable according to the prevailing production patterns.

Gabriel García Márquez's *One Hundred Years of Solitude*, which describes the construction of large estates in Macondo with this method, is fundamental to an understanding of Colombian history:

Only when they had coffee did Arcadio reveal the purpose
of his visit: He had received a complaint against José Arcadio.
It was said that he began plowing his patio and had continued straight for the adjoining lands, knocking down fences
and destroying ranches with his cattle, until he forcefully
took possession of the best pieces of the area's land. As for
the farmers who were not stripped of their lands because
their lands were of no interest to him, every Saturday he
demanded that they pay him an amount and went accompanied by bulldogs and a double-barreled shotgun. He didn't
deny it. He based his right to do so under the premise that
the seized lands had been distributed by José Arcadio
Buendía during the times of the foundation.[2]

In 1948, the assassination of populist leader Jorge Eliécer
Gaitán unleashed a violent period that lasted twenty years and
took a heavy toll on the population: 300,000 civilians died and
more than two million were forced to flee.[3] While there had
been uprisings by farmers and other violent incidents in various
regions before, this period erased all prior regional characteristics
and spread violence to vast areas of the country. In Valle, Tolima,
and Cauca, vast areas of farmland wound up in the hands of
estate owners and businessmen. In the 1950s, at the start of the
period called *La Violencia* (The Violence), farmers were expelled
from the best lands and valleys and forced into urban areas or
toward farmland borders and colonization areas—where low
incomes, lack of infrastructure and markets, and pressure from
large landowners caused farmers to live in permanently precari-
ous conditions—mainly in the south and in the Amazon jungle.
In Urabá in the mid-1950s, when the road to the sea was opened
and the land was appraised, the farmers who had cleared the
jungle and planted the first banana trees were forced to sell their
land well below market value or abandon it. Only fifteen people

out of 5,000 were granted deeds to their land at that time. The others were condemned to make their way through the jungle.[4]

Large landowners advocated expanding farmland borders. As Molano states, "Colonization in Colombia has been a way to expand large estates and, therefore, a permanent displacement process encouraged by settlers, which has contributed to the gradual extinction of the jungle."[5]

Colonization areas became the breeding ground for illicit crops, which would at least ensure the farmers' survival. Moreover, bordering areas' lack of institutional development and reserve in the state created a framework favorable to conflict resolution via violent means, for property rights or any other issue. In these vast areas where the state is weak, the armed opposition converges with the landless farmers, that is, the political and the social conflicts.

During this period, large estates expanded and Liberal or Conservative Party supporters (depending on who had the military upper hand at the time) settled throughout many areas. More than 300,000 ownership deeds changed hands during those years. Migration from rural areas to the towns occurred during this time as well, thereby transforming Colombia into an urban society. This demographic change, which took place faster than it had in other societies, occurred for the most part between the 1950s and the 1960s. Bogotá's population, which in 1951 registered 715,220 inhabitants, reached 1.6 million in 1964. Today, 73 percent of the total population lives in urban areas. Until the 1940s, the proportions were reversed; over a period of five decades, Colombian demographics did a complete U-turn. As this transformation was not accompanied by an industrialization process that could justify such dramatic migrations toward urban areas, one can deduce that these demographic changes were caused by violence carried out for political gains.

In the 1970s, another large population of displaced people flowed into colonized areas and towns. Economic policies aimed at eliminating obstacles to foreign investment, introduced by then-president Misael Pastrana (1970–74), decreased the incomes of small farmers and led large estates to merge with commercial agriculture. Some farmers joined the working class, while others fled to colonized areas and towns. Moreover, tough counter-insurgency policies were implemented, and paramilitary groups emerged to confront the growing presence of left-wing guerrilla groups (descendents of the Liberal self-defense groups formed during *La Violencia* period). In Magdalena Medio, the actions perpetrated by the *Masetos*—whose name is derived from the para-military group Muerte a Secuestradores (Death to Kidnappers)—generated an exodus to Barrancabermeja of farmers who left behind large land territories.

The absence of the state in vast areas of the country has con-tributed to the creation of de facto states, which are controlled by actors other than the Colombian state who impose their own rules. Illicit drug-related economics played an important role in the spread and overall use of violence: in many places, local authori-ties were reorganized, assisted by the fact that large territories were increasingly owned by drug traffickers. In 1997, according to the Colombian Agrarian Reform Institute (INCORA—Instituto Colombiano de Reforma Agraria), these landowners held 4 million hectares of mostly flat, high-quality land used for stockbreeding.[6] The political and economic power of these groups further complicated the already existing violence as dif-ferent and changing alliances continued to succeed one another. In conflict areas with drug estates, drug traffickers created and supported paramilitary groups to fight guerrillas (associating themselves with some sectors of the armed forces). In other areas, the tax system imposed by the guerrillas upon these activities was used to generate income, and drug traffickers benefited by using the guerillas to contain military and police actions. Clearly, the actors have changing interests and alliances, depending on the region and the dynamics of the conflict in question.

The only difference between the current situation and what occurred in previous periods is the extent and magnitude of the phenomenon. As the number of regions and actors involved increases, the amount of space and possible solutions decreases.[7] Moreover, the lines separating the various armed groups are constantly changing, and, as a result, when they operate in distant zones from their bases, these areas can go from the control of one actor to another without warning. Residents of these communities are guaranteed to undergo some form of terror when power in their area changes hands, as they will most definitely be accused of supporting the previous controlling actor or defeated party.

In many cases, the only choice left for community residents is to flee to the so-called shantytowns on the peripheries of the big cities, where anonymity and a certain degree of security are usually guaranteed. There, displaced people assimilate and become mere numbers on never-ending urban poverty lists, contributing to the concealment of the problem and the prevention of addressing or even acknowledging its real causes.

Neoliberal model of pressure

Besides the traditional pressure, based on violence, exerted by the local political and economic elite, new factors have arisen. The elite have now entered into an alliance with multinational credit institutions and capital assets, which requires an expansion of capital circuits, bestows privileges upon capital assets, strengthens the economy's primary sector (agricultural industry) through foreign markets, promotes foreign investment and exports, and toughens repression against social protests.

The events during *La Violencia* gave rise to capital accumulation in the second half of the twentieth century. Violence has now increased in the areas of new capital circuit expansion, where development macro-projects are implemented, where illicit crops are grown, or in areas rich in biodiversity and natural resources. The methods used to expand the development model aim to connect regions in the periphery with the main centers around the country and to strengthen the means of communication with world markets. The Development Plan of the Pastrana administration envisaged the construction of eight transversal highways and eight main highways, plus railways, as well as air, ferry, and sea transportation and communications. The purpose was to guarantee multinationals and private investors access to the country's resources.

Colombia has more than 30 million hectares of non-commercially controlled forests of usable timber. The government is promoting the exploitation of a forest corridor south of the Meta River and encouraging national and foreign investment. The Orinoco-Meta River project, jointly financed by the Japanese and Colombian governments, plans to build canals, ports, and tolls, and to give concessions to a transnational company. The indigenous Sikuani, Sáliva, and Achagua communities, who live on the shores of the Meta River, report that they have not been consulted on this project.[8]

Displaced Afro-Colombian communities living on the

Cacarica River Basin (known as Chocó) have reported on the illegal deforestation of their land by the company YIRH, which operates in conjunction with the logging company Maderas del Darién. Its activities go unnoticed, even when they do not respect environmental regulations, due to their influence on the body in charge of granting concessions and to their longtime protection by the paramilitaries. This area has the largest *cativo* forest in the country. The Chocó region also provides 70 percent of the total national production of raw materials for the food industry, 18 percent of gold, and 13.8 percent of silver; bauxite, manganese, tin, chromium, and nickel beds, as well as oil fields, are all found in its soil.[9]

In Chocó ("the best corner in America"), there are hydro-electric, port-building, and interoceanic projects, oil lines, roads, and railways. The value of this land and its opening to trade explains the war against the area's communities: agricultural industries based in Urabá (Antioquia) will be transferred to this area, oil fields and mine exploration will be started here soon, and a large hydroelectric project will be developed that will allow the export of energy to Central America and the United States. Some French multinationals in the area are already extracting genetic materials and medicinal plants.

Other multinationals, such as the oil-drilling companies, are very interested in ensuring their presence in Colombia and in performing their activities in a "safe" environment. In 1997, Britain's *Guardian* newspaper reported on British Petroleum's involvement in financing paramilitaries. It is also known that Occidental Petroleum exerted pressure on the U.S. Congress to expand Plan Colombia's scope from the Putumayo region (as previously planned) to areas where the company has interests.

For guerrilla groups, the control of land translates into a widening of their sources of income by means of taxing all economic activities carried out in the area by either national actors or foreign companies. For paramilitary groups and the state's armed forces, the aim is to guarantee the implementation of these economic activities and to eliminate possible "obstacles." In exchange, those who are protected pay a tax and finance these groups.

The interests at stake

The conflict's armed actors use displacement within the framework of struggles for territorial control of strategic areas: from a military perspective, to control corridors or those areas used for the trafficking of weapons and/or the transport of illegal products; from a political perspective, to destroy the enemy's real or potential social bases. For example, the paramilitary groups and the state use displacement in regions that support a significant presence of social actors and a tradition of organization in the form of unions, farmers' associations, and/or indigenous organizations. This is sometimes accompanied by a structured repopulation plan. In Cauca, important indigenous organizations, grouped under Cauca's Regional Indigenous Council (CRIC— Consejo Regional Indígena del Cauca), have fought to be granted collective land deeds and to create indigenous safeguards. In 2001, there were 60 such deeds totaling 120,000 hectares. These communities are strongly rooted in the land and intend to keep their customs, language, and territory linked to their traditional activities, i.e., they are "withdrawing from the neoliberal model, seeking to prove that another model is feasible."[10] All armed actors have their eyes on this region, as it is considered strategically crucial in determining the course of the war due to its mountainous topography and organizational and fighting traditions. Yet, displacements are also generated in wealthy areas by the struggle for control over land and natural resources.[11] Depending on the region, displacements take place in areas sought after for export-oriented stockbreeding or one-crop farming exploitation (such as African palm or the banana industry in Urabá); where mega-projects (e.g., Atrato-Truandó interoceanic canal in Chocó) are planned; where land has been appraised based upon foreign investment plans (road, port, and air projects); where energy and natural resources are extracted (gold in San Lucas Hill Country, oil in indigenous U'wa territory, hydroelectric dams in Chocó); and where illicit crops are cultivated. Moreover, acts of force for purely strategic or political ends and disputes over regional political reorganization or over the control of regional governments also play a role.[12]

According to a study carried out by the Solidarity Network, the regions that account for 84 percent of the country's displacement figures also account for 78 percent of its oil revenues. Nevertheless, these regions have poverty rates that exceed the country's average. Forced migrations take place in areas where people are not politically active, as shown in their electoral participation, but are very socially active through means such as protests and demonstrations, which make the high social costs of the displacements evident.[13] Selective displacement also occurs based on threats against and extrajudicial executions of social leaders, such as union representatives, journalists, human rights activists, professors, etc.

Regarding public or private development mega-projects, especially those related to energy and communication infrastructures, the mere announcement of their introduction affects the value of the lands, which then become a target of debate. When people flee, local landowners or multinational companies (and the alliances among them and other actors) can then appropriate these abandoned lands or buy them at very low costs. This is extremely easy in colonization areas where land deeds do not exist (for instance, 80–85 percent of the land in Putumayo is not registered). Even where deeds do exist, farmers can find without notice that their deeds are no longer valid because they have been granted to other owners. Moreover, the populations who remain in these areas are left without social organizations, which are "shut down" to prevent the affected people from protesting or complaining, thereby protecting the interests of those participating in the prospective infrastructure construction operation.

In Middle and Lower Atrato, only two weeks after the plans for the Atrato-Truandó interoceanic canal project were announced, land prices skyrocketed; two months later paramilitary groups appeared on the scene to intimidate the area's local population and force them to leave. Gradually, those who left were replaced by new settlers who were more supportive of "the cause."

In Simití, Southern Bolívar, a region where several gold-digging companies operate, murders and disappearances caused by the military and paramilitaries—and by fighting between the latter and the ELN guerrilla group—have caused displacements. The largest gold mines in Latin America are located in the San Lucas Hill Country area and produce 42 percent of all of the gold in Colombia. For years the gold digging had been carried out by 35,000 miners affiliated with the Southern Bolívar Farmers' and Miners' Association (ASOAGROMISBOL—Asociación de Agricultores y Mineros del Sur de Bolívar), by means of mining committees. Currently, there are forty-five committees with collective licenses to exploit various mines. However, the company San Lucas Ltd. (associated with a Canadian firm) claims ownership rights to exploit all of the mines located throughout the territory, as the government has granted this company a seventy-year license. The ongoing irregularities reported by the miners' association have caused massacres and selective assassinations of mining leaders, as well as massive incursions from the paramilitary in the area since 1998. The region is also a strategic landmark, as it has been proposed as a "goodwill" area where negotiations between the government and the ELN are likely to take place.

These examples demonstrate how the lines that guide the expansion activities of armed actors are closely linked to the country's economy and to extraction activities. The socioeconomic development model is related to conflict and displacement because the exclusion of large sectors of the population is a source of conflict and violence and because the models imposed by national and multinational companies only worsen existing problems.

The issue of farming

The economic development model in Colombia has been derived from, among other influences, the theories of Lauchlin Currie, a French-speaking Canadian International Monetary Fund economist,[14] who recommended a reduction in the number of farmers, and stressed the economic importance of agriculture as a means to accelerate development in a country. As had other development supporters before him, Currie believed that economic efficacy depended on encouraging the exodus of farmers, especially the less competitive farmers within the market; however, Currie took this concept even further, recommending a model that deliberately accelerated this process by triggering emigration from rural areas. Should conditions not be favorable for implementing this model, war could be used as a means to generate the same results. The 1972 Chicoral Agreement and the end of land reform at the beginning of the 1970s was founded on the notion of a "modern" countryside based on large capitalist and highly mechanized estates as a key to development.

In Colombia, the expulsion of farmers was not accompanied by an industrialization model capable of absorbing this new labor force; legal and illegal measures had to be taken to control social movements, guarantee social stability, and protect foreign investment interests. The National Front (1958–78) and the alternating governments between the two traditional parties made up the strategy to guarantee this stability and prevent other social and political sectors from participating.

The semi-feudal land-ownership and power model has been replaced by a neoliberal model that confronts indigenous farming economies with major national farming and stockbreeding interests, and with world economies (opening borders), as well as finance capital, mega-projects, and transnational investments. These projects are considered crucial for the development model. The measures to guarantee their implementation involve the expropriation of, among others, farm, indigenous, and black communities living in these territories, who are considered a nuisance.

As pointed out by the Colombian Episcopal Conference, "Connecting forced displacement and the agrarian conflict uncovers the interests that use the uprooting of peoples as an economic and cheaper way to achieve their objectives, i.e. accumulating ready-to-use and therefore more valuable land."[15]

A census carried out by the National Farmers Association

(ANUC—Asociación Nacional de Usuarios Campesinos) revealed that, of 15.5 million farmers in 1990, at least 5 million left their lands or had given up traditional farming at some point during the preceding decade. This meant that 1.7 million hectares of farmland were abandoned and occupied for the most part by armed actors—occupying wastelands as part of their strategy—and by large or medium estate owners who used terror to buy land at undervalued prices or to acquire the deeds of abandoned farms. As Carlos Baquero, a social researcher, noted, "In 1990 alone, after the massacres perpetrated in villages and the countryside, there were more land deeds transferred than in the first forty years of the twentieth century."[16]

Political economy of war, poverty, and exclusion

Within the globalized framework, which imposes the reduction of state structures and economic measures that provoke the exclusion of large social sectors, other actors appear on the scene and initiate or enter legal or illegal economic networks to guarantee their survival, threatening sometimes even the state itself or fighting to attain sovereignty. Consequently, in fragile or weak states, there is a tendency toward illegality, which can turn war into a lifestyle in order to generate income. Ongoing crises are "not the result of irrational actions but are economic organizational tools of a power,"[17] even when hidden behind other justifications. In terms of fighting for resources and goods, war means exclusion and elimination of the "other," in that, "it is not meant to earn people's hearts and minds but to expel or eliminate them."

Numerous authors have studied complex modern armed conflicts and their relationship with globalization and the process of the breakdown or weakening of state structures in various places throughout the world. Some even affirm that these conflicts have more to do with other forms of organized armed violence, such as organized crime and Mafia networks, than with traditional wars. Many of the conflicts give rise to strong illegal economies that grow faster and are stronger than legal ones, for instance, the uncontrolled exploitation of diamonds, timber, and oil within the framework of several African conflicts.[18] In Colombia, the political economy of war has allowed the various actors to consolidate and obtain more benefits from war than they would ever obtain from peace, within a framework marked by a complete absence of institutional authorities in large areas of the country, the state's inability to solve conflicts and settle social disputes, and by the elite's patrimonial use of the state.

Drug-trafficking activities, abductions, extortion, and "revolutionary taxes" on economic activities, etc., finance guerrillas. Despite their initial resistance to illicit crops, the guerrillas established a tax system affecting drug traffickers, intermediaries, transportation, and farmworkers. State employees also benefit from the conflict by inflating budgetary proposals and taking contributions from multinational companies that require protection, as well as profiting from their political (influencing state policies) and social (status) roles. Their broad powers are a guarantee of their impunity. They have also benefited from funds allocated to fight guerrillas and from the proliferation of private security firms, which are often managed by retired military officers.[19] Other actors benefiting from this situation are the paramilitaries and the elite who, throughout history, have used violence to control land and assets and who consider guerrillas to be a threat to the implementation of neoliberal policies that would allow them to increase their profits.

The war economy was estimated to be 13 percent of the country's gross national product in 1995. It directly affected 5–6 percent of the total Colombian population and indirectly affected 10–13 percent of it.[20] Under the circumstances, certain data should be taken into consideration. For example, in the year 2000, Colombia had 42.3 million inhabitants, of whom 73 percent lived in urban areas.[21] The lower class amounted to 62 percent of the total population, 33 percent were middle class (gradually decreasing), and wealth and power were in the hands of 5 percent of the overall population. Since 1991, all socio-economic layers, except the highest classes, have fallen down the social ladder, expanding the gap between incomes of the elite and those of the lower classes.

The unemployment rate amounts to 21 percent in urban areas, where underemployment reaches 28 percent and youth unemployment is 50 percent among the lowest classes. Nevertheless, we must highlight the fact that in Colombia those working for more than one hour a day are considered employed, as long as the job is stable. The fact that more than 1.6 million children work[22] constitutes a serious problem, as a lack of childcare and schooling are key poverty-generating mechanisms. In 2000, poverty was estimated to affect 61.5 percent of the population. This figure reached 49.5 percent in urban areas and as high as 84.9 percent in rural areas. Economic surplus accumulates in 3 percent of the population.

The population cannot benefit from expenditure hikes on basic services and education, which are limited by neoliberal economic policies and by the prevalence of finance capital. The Colombian state's military spending went from 1.6 percent of the gross domestic product (GDP) in 1985 to 2.9 percent in 2002.

Meanwhile, social spending, which had doubled between 1985 and 1996, decreased from 16.7 percent to 10 percent of the GDP between 1996 and 2002. If the conflict continues to worsen, military spending could exceed 5 percent of the GDP at the end of this decade, which would make it even more difficult to invest in human priorities. In addition, it is estimated that the conflict causes an annual loss of approximately 2 percent of the GDP.[23]

It is clear that economic, social, and political exclusion and poverty polarize the atmosphere and strengthen the decision to use violence as an option, while violence and the growing number of conflict scenarios also aggravate and increase economic imbalances.

The problem of figures

The Consultancy on Human Rights and Displacement (CODHES—Consultoria para los Derechos Humanos y el Desplazamiento) estimates the number of displaced to have been more than 340,000 in 2001 and more than 400,000 in 2002. Other organizations, such as the Colombian Bishops' Conference (Pastoral Social), the Red Cross, and the government's Social Solidarity Network, provide widely different estimates of the number of displaced based on their differing methodologies for counting.

Some characteristics to highlight:

- The crisis is especially important in Antioquia, Bolívar, Santander, Córdoba, Magdalena, Chocó, Cesar, Sucre, Meta, Putumayo, Valle del Cauca, Caquetá, Cauca, Guaviare, Nariño, and Arauca. Antioquia alone represents 25 percent of the national total of displaced.

- Farmers and black and indigenous communities are especially affected, although the "political cleansing" phenomenon, and murders of and threats against union leaders, political and human rights activists, community leaders, journalists, teachers, health workers, etc., have increased displacements among these groups.

- All systems of estimates agree on the high incidence of forced displacement among people under eighteen years of age, who comprise nearly half of the displaced population.

- Although the main trend is urban-rural displacement, intra-urban displacement is on the rise with people migrating to large urban areas fleeing from security threats and seeking new survival strategies. Thirty-seven families are estimated to arrive in Bogotá every day.[24]

- Despite a majority of individual or family displacements, the number of mass displacements (more than ten families or fifty people at a time) seems to be on the rise. In 1997, for the first time in Colombia, two displacement camps were opened: one in Pavarandó (Antioquia) and another in the Turbo stadium, where people spent more than two years. In June and July 1998, 10,000 people in seventeen municipalities were displaced to Barrancabermeja.

- Though guerrillas participate in more acts of displacement, their interventions affect fewer people. Paramilitaries, through a terror-oriented communication strategy, carry out more effective actions in terms of numbers: it is estimated that each massacre they perpetrate causes 170 people to flee. Some analysts point out that massacres, violence, and brutality against human beings are linked to memories of experiences from *La Violencia,* thus transporting people back in time and playing tricks on their imaginations.

From the war against drugs to the war against terrorism[25]

The conflict in Colombia escalated during the 1990s due to, among other factors, the rapid increase in drug trafficking, from which all of the armed actors and several social sectors benefited. This, until recently, is precisely the area in which American intervention has been focused in Colombia: within the framework of the war against drugs, programs to forcibly eradicate illicit crops are applied, and programs to aid the Colombian government, mostly in terms of military activities, are implemented, which translates into increased militarization of the society and the spread of the conflict. These forced eradication strategies provoke new population displacements and intensify the settlement process, thus contributing to broadening the agricultural borders. Along with the fact that they are mostly applied in areas controlled by the guerrillas, this has led some analysts to declare that Plan Colombia is the "armed wing" of the Free Trade Area of the Americas (FTAA) and is useful for the economic model since it facilitates agrarian reform, the concentration of lands, and development based on exclusion. "The FTAA project is in keeping with the same logic of Plan Colombia, conceived to control the area where Central and South America meet, a region that is especially rich in oil and neighbors the Amazon, which is rich in natural resources, water, and biodiversity."[26]

The antidrug strategy in Colombia is based on a "double discourse." On the one hand, this country is the principal producer and provides 90 percent of the cocaine that is demanded by the American market, which makes the eradication of the crops an issue of national security for Washington. On the other hand—taking into account that drug trafficking is one of the primary sources of income for the armed groups—eliminating this illicit economy would cut off the funds of the armed actors and make it possible for the conflict to be brought to an end. However, both of these premises are mistaken. As Alfredo Molano wrote:

> Drug trafficking is not the cause of our ills, but, rather, it is one of its most dramatic manifestations. The problem dates

back even prior to the country's drug trade and is more complex. It originates from a social and political structure that reproduces and increases economic inequalities and prevents democratic opposition against this situation. It is the same matrix of armed conflict, institutional corruption, and violence. Attempting to destroy drug trafficking without attacking its roots, or by going about it tangentially, is a useless ploy.[27]

The Colombian conflict has gone on for more than forty years, and its roots precede and are different from those of drug trafficking.

The inequity of the possession of the land and wealth, the weakness and corruption of the state (despite having a sophisticated legal structure), the agrarian *caudillismo,* the isolation of some of the country's regions from others— which impeded the configuration of a centralized state—the intolerance among groups with conflicting interests and the lack of space for political participation of broad sectors of the population are all factors that are found at the roots of the conflict. The drug trafficking made it worse."[28]

Molano also wrote:

The illicit crops arrived to Colombia at the hands of the drug traffickers and their international networks. They found a miserable peasantry, some corrupt authorities that were easy to bribe, a political class that was eager to obtain resources in exchange for impunity, and a business class accustomed to easy work and abundant profits. The perfect setting for their prosperity.[29]

With the implementation of eradication programs in producer countries Bolivia and Peru and the interception of transport planes, cultivation in Colombia began. This situation benefited from Colombia's particular conditions: it had a state that did not control major parts of its territory and a model of land occupation based on unregulated settlement. It is calculated that 62 percent of Colombia's coca exploitations are fewer than three hectares each and are run by small farmers. The coca option must be understood within the framework of the rural economic crisis, the absence of transportation and market infrastructures, and the high levels of rural poverty. Coca, in this context, is the only economically profitable product.

The easy money from drug trafficking has worsened the war because the major cash flow associated with trafficking has allowed all of the armed groups to finance themselves, either by controlling the business or charging a "toll fee" to the intermediaries who come to purchase cocaine's *pasta* base. Sectors of the state and the banking, industrial, and financial systems also participate, which in turn exacerbates the corruption. The various actors involved have driven the massive sale of arms and led to the creation of new private armies that defend the interests of the major drug traffickers, constituting a new source of violence.[30]

The principal path of the internationalization of the Colombian conflict is American intervention, which was limited until 2002 to drug trafficking. Colombia has been a major recipient of American aid for years within the framework of Washington's war against drugs. Since 2000, the greater part of this aid has been classified within the so-called Plan Colombia. This plan, approved during the Clinton administration, signifies an investment of billions of U.S. dollars toward the fight against drugs. It combines a section directed at the forced eradication of illicit crops (80 percent of the total funds) with aid for social and economic programs that would make the substitution of these crops possible (the remaining 20 percent). Its final objective is to train, finance, and supply armaments and consultants to the antidrug battalions of the army that work in Southern Colombia, an area where an estimated 60 percent of the country's coca crops are produced. The principal instrument used on the ground is massive air fumigation with chemical substances aimed at ending the region's production.[31] Such fumigation is protected by the army's antidrug battalions, trained and armed by the United States.

The fumigation of coca and poppy plantations is not new in Colombia. It has been carried out since 1978, with different criteria and at different rates. The new feature presented in Plan Colombia was the number of hectares to be fumigated and the chemical mixture: a new and more effective concentration of Roundup (Roundup Ultra), a commercial mixture based in glyphosate herbicide. Additives, such as Cosmo-Flux 411F, are part of this mixture, which improves the product's adherence to the plants. The average dosage is 23.66 liters per hectare, which contains more than 10 liters of Roundup Ultra. There are no studies on the effects of this formula on human health or the environment;[32] however, the populations of the affected areas report respiratory and skin infections, congenital malformations, etc., as well as serious contamination of the land and water. Agricultural workers are forced to flee because the ground becomes unusable for agriculture.

Colombia uses more herbicides in the fight against illicit crops than any other country, and it destroys the most hectares of illegal plantations in the world. However, demand for illicit drugs has unyieldingly continued to increase, and their cultivation, processing, and traffic in recent years have reached unprecedented levels.[33] Colombia continues to be the principal producer and provides the vast majority of the cocaine that the American market demands, despite the fact that, since 1996, more than a half a million hectares have been fumigated. In 2003, the first surface reduction was registered; however, this was compensated, to some extent, by an increase in Peru and Bolivia.[34] This is the other mistaken premise in Washington's strategy: while demand remains stable, production will continue, whether in Colombia or somewhere else. The cultivated area of coca remains stable in the Andean region, around 200,000 hectares in the last ten years.[35]

Clearly, Washington's strategy is condemned to failure. The air fumigation programs attack the weakest link in the drug chain—farmers and settlers. They do not attack the major drug traffickers or other key aspects of the business, such as consumption, money laundering by drug traffickers in international financial circuits, or the import of the chemical precursors needed to prepare cocaine or heroin from the coca or poppy leaf—90 percent of which are produced by American and European companies. At the same time, fumigation has strong ecological and social effects, besides contributing to the militarization of the country and the worsening of the conflict. The peasants whose farms are fumigated must abandon them and search for new areas to settle or go to the cities. The movement of crops implies the extension of the conflict, since armed actors move to areas with new crops and begin to exercise control over the population using tactics that involve violations of human rights and International Humanitarian Law (IHL). Moreover, the exodus toward the cities means that the long list of displacements and excluded populations will grow even longer.

Meanwhile, deforestation continues to increase and the agricultural borders continue to expand, while in the "cleared territories," the resources that have not been affected by the fumigations can be exploited (e.g., the oil in Putumayo). Territorial control allows for the exclusive dominance of these resources and the construction of communication channels to export them to the developed countries.

> In this sense, the militarization of the territory is focused on discouraging any type of resistance. As a matter of fact, there is a confluence of spaces between the regional interests in Latin America and the location of the current and future American bases ... and the strengthening of Plan Colombia, the target of struggle of many Andean organizations that claim the main sources of violence are the same regions that are the richest in biodiversity."[36]

The conjunction of Uribe's "democratic security" with Bush's "war against terrorism"

Successive Colombian administrations have always accepted, with varying levels of enthusiasm or opposition, the antidrug policy imposed by the United States. They have also simultaneously fought the war against insurgent movements in scenarios ranging from direct military confrontation to open dialogue in search of a negotiated end to the conflict and reinsertion.

The last negotiation process took place between the Andrés Pastrana government and the FARC. Its collapse in February 2002, along with the changes that took place in the international arena after September 11, 2001, were capitalized on by the presidential candidate Álvaro Uribe, who won the elections with a program based on winning the war against insurgent groups. The "democratic security" policy that he has used to achieve this end since becoming president in August 2002 translates into reforms aimed at cutting public liberties and procedural laws; giving more power to security forces; reducing the legal powers of authorities, such as the constitutional court and the public defender; and involving civilians in the conflict by creating patrols run by "peasant soldiers." In order to win the war, Uribe acts under the illusion that there is no war; rather, there is a "struggle by the legitimate state against groups of terrorists that finance their actions from the earnings they gain from drug trafficking."[37]

This vision of the conflict has several negative consequences: it polarizes the society and criminalizes dissidents; it rejects the structural causes of the conflict; it ignores IHL (by considering that there is no conflict); and it heightens the country's human rights crisis by weakening the international accords and treaties signed by Colombia, such as the antiterrorist statute that grants judicial authority to military forces. Last, it makes the possibility of a negotiated peace even more distant given that negotiations with terrorists do not occur.[38] Civil-society groups, human rights organizations, unions, and members of the political opposition parties are accused of supporting terrorism and subversion if they express disagreement with the president's policies or attempt to promote alternatives or respect for human rights. This condition makes them even more vulnerable to threats and murder.[39] All in all, these policies are driving Colombian society to become more radical and violent.[40]

Uribe informed the American administration of his objectives by means of a letter addressed to President George W. Bush on September 19, 2002. Among the objectives were

- establishment of policies aimed at eliminating the cultivation, processing, and trafficking of illicit drugs and strengthening the state and the rule of law throughout all Colombian territory, especially in areas under the control of the illegal armed groups

- reforms in the budget and personnel of the Colombian armed forces
- funding for more resources to achieve these objectives
- programs to support sustainable rural development

The new president asked for American support for his strategy, and immediately after Uribe sent the letter, Bush signed the National Security Presidential Directive 18 relating to military aid to Colombia. Among its objectives were to continue assistance to combat illicit drugs and terrorism, defend human rights, and promote development; provide aid, advice, training, and intelligence support to the Colombian armed forces and the police; encourage growth and development through support of the market economy and implementation of the FTAA; reduce the production and trafficking of cocaine and heroine by strengthening antidrug programs; and support the growth and professionalization of Colombian security forces.[41] This policy signifies a clear break with Clinton's Guideline 73, which limited American aid to the fight against drugs.

U.S. involvement increases

Colombia is now one of the Latin American countries that Washington is most interested in because of drug trafficking, oil, proximity to Hugo Chávez's Venezuela, its geopolitical location in terms of the Caribbean, Central America, and the Andes, and its vicinity to Panamá and the Canal, whose stability is considered key in the region. Washington views the Colombian crisis as the principal threat to security in the hemisphere. It is considered a laboratory where the most serious problems of the current international arena come together: terrorist groups, drug trafficking and illicit activities that can finance terrorist acts, and huge territories without state control.

Colombia was already a major recipient of American military aid before September 11. Nevertheless, during the Clinton administration, there was constant tension between the U.S. State and Defense Departments. The former affirmed that Plan Colombia was an antidrug plan, while the latter maintained that the lines between drug trafficker and guerrilla were weak and that the plan needed to include an anti-insurgent component. (It even coined the concept of "ambiguous war" to justify such an approach.[42]) As of September 11, 2001, this conflict ended, and the Bush administration eliminated prior restrictions and reconsidered its military aid as an instrument to fight against drug trafficking in order to link it to the fight against insurgents, and, especially, to be able to classify it within the terms of the global war against terrorism.

The American official in charge of the fight against drugs, John P. Walters, recently affirmed that the antidrug war should be bound to the war against terrorism since "violence and terror are associated with the drug trade."[43] Walters praised Uribe for his "unprecedented" efforts to put an end to drug trafficking. Moreover, Walters believes that Uribe's is the model that the governments of Bolivia and Peru—countries that also receive American aid—should follow. Not only has the line between the war against drugs and the war against insurgents been broken, but at the moment, Washington has more troops and civil contractors on Colombian soil than ever before. The military personnel went from 117 members in November 2001 to 358 members in May 2003.[44]

According to Center for International Policy data from

October 2003, American aid to Colombia totaled $2.4 billion between 2000 and 2003, more than 80 percent of which was directed to the Colombian armed forces and police. A new large sum of money, exceeding $688 million, has been requested from Congress for 2004,with the same proportion of military aid as before.[45] In total, this translates into more than $1.6 million a day in military aid. In July 2003, Congress debated Bush's petition to approve the Andean Regional Initiative. This would allocate $731 million to seven countries in the area, in order to "support a campaign against drug trafficking and against the activities of organizations deemed as terrorists in Colombia."

In the face of this situation, the European Union (EU) and its members maintain positions that oscillate between cooperating in economic development projects—distancing themselves from the military solution—and joining the United States in its antiterrorist discourse. In general, the stance that the EU and the European Community countries have maintained until now has been to encourage peace through negotiations and to focus their support on development projects and humanitarian aid, especially for the displaced.

The worsening of the war and the humanitarian crisis

More concerned with other priorities in foreign policy, such as the situation in Iraq, and caught up in the global antiterrorism discourse, the authorities in Washington have opted for an approach to the Colombian conflict not based on an analysis of its complexity, but rather on increasing military aid and situating it within the global war on terror, while at the same time reducing the demands and conditions related to human rights.[46] The presidents of the United States and Colombia agree on making the use of force a priority, a policy that is already weakening international commitments to human rights and IHL. The antiterrorist statute that came into effect in June 2004 in Colombia allows authorities to intercept or search private communications, without previous legal warrant, and make arrests and house searches of people who are suspected of possibly preparing terrorist acts. Moreover, the attorney general can create, in places where there is no judicial authority, special units of the judicial police with members of the armed forces that can be turned to at a moment's notice.[47] This contradicts the International Pact on Civil and Political Rights and the American Convention on Human Rights, and has been highly criticized by the UN High Commission on Human Rights, the Inter-American Commission on Human Rights, the UN High Commissioner for Human Rights, and, in Colombia, by the constitutional court and the attorney general's office. The demobilization of paramilitary groups has also been criticized, as there is no legal basis to pardon drug-trafficking crimes and serious human rights violations, and because it is not clear how such reinsertion into civil society will be carried out. The spectacle of the demobilization of the first 850 paramilitaries in November 2003 was characterized by Human Rights Watch as "an exhibition of impunity."

The humanitarian crisis in Colombia, coupled with the application of these policies in 2003, highlights complex trends. The figures regarding violence remain very high, although there are major differences between the official figures and those provided by human rights NGOs. According to the Center for Popular Research and Education (CINEP—Centro de Investigación y Educación Popular), 4,351 people were victims of human rights violations between July 1, 2002, and June 30,

2003, especially arbitrary arrests (2,546), extrajudicial executions (792), and threats (573).[48] The trends are contradictory: the threats, homicides, kidnappings, and number of civilians killed in military actions, among other things, decreased during this period, while arbitrary arrests increased by 400 percent. In August 2003, for example, massive arrests took place in several cities, allegedly for connections with the guerrillas. All those who were imprisoned were freed after three months for lack of evidence. In addition, "disappearances" have increased dramatically. According to the Association of Families of Detainees and Missing Persons (ASFADDES—Asociación de Familiares de Detenidos y Desaparecidos), 3,593 people "disappeared" between 2002 and 2003, even more than disappeared between 1994 and 2001, in acts that were, for the most part, attributed to the state's security forces and the paramilitaries.[49]

Hidden behind the statistics are the new dynamics in which the armed conflict unfolds. The FARC have withdrawn into areas of the country where they still have a strong presence and carry out acts of sabotage and attacks against infrastructure (electrical installations, pipelines, etc.), including some in cities. As for the paramilitaries, although the data is debatable, the agreements with the government to demobilize have led to a certain reduction in the massacres in exchange for other modus operandi. Meanwhile, during Uribe's administration, they have managed to deploy themselves throughout a large part of the territory and to control areas that used to belong to the guerrillas, which might have allowed them to reduce actions against civilians, the main victims in the fight for territory.

The latest data from CODHES shows that a population of approximately 175,270 people was displaced between January and

September 2003, which signifies a decrease of about 49 percent with respect to the same period in 2002.[50] To explain the decrease, CODHES points to a change in strategy by the armed actors, who have now opted to control the civilian population through armed sieges in many areas. This new strategy of confinement may involve the siege of whole communities and the control of the entrances and exits to territories, selective blockades, limits on access to health services, and delivery of humanitarian assistance. Therefore, it would be a different manifestation than that of Colombia's humanitarian crisis, which "shows that the strategies that turn the civilian population into a resource of war continue to be in effect; however, they are expressed in a different manner."[51]

CODHES believes that other factors also influence this decrease in the number of displacements: for example, the civil resistance of some communities to move; the deployment and apparent restructuring of the guerrillas' strategy against the offensive of the armed forces; the truce by paramilitary groups in talks with the government and their new forms of operation (selective murders and individual displacements instead of massacres); the increase of subregistration in all of the monitoring systems due to threats against victims of the conflict's armed actors if they declare their displacement status; the skepticism of the displaced toward the aid that they will receive from the state; and the invisibility of the issue in the media, "which demonstrates its fatigue with regard to a problem that tends to become chronic and repetitive."[52]

Hundreds of thousands of people continue to be expelled within the framework of the growth of the armed conflict, the strategies of the forced eradication of illicit crops (which are increasingly an integral part of the conflict), and the implementation of an exclusionary and greedy economic development model. According to CODHES, around 30,000 people were expelled by the fumigations of illicit crops (mostly in Putumayo, Caquetá, Guaviare, Northern Santander, and César). The country has accumulated nearly 3 million displaced people, and the territorial reorganization of power as well as the economic structure continues.

Conclusions

Forced displacement is a phenomenon linked to the history of Colombia and to the country's unfinished historical processes. The economic and political elite have used displacement to "homogenize" the population in a given area and to maintain and expand large estates. Currently, the pressure exerted by the neo-liberal model to increase capital circuits has made the process more difficult by introducing factors that change the value of the land. As such, people are not displaced "by violence"; rather, violence is the tool used to expel the population. The true causes for displacement are hidden behind the violence. The reasons for displacement include strategic control of military and political areas, restructuring of local and regional powers, control or disruption of social movements, control of production and extraction activities (of natural resources and minerals), mega-projects, expansion of stockbreeding estates and agricultural industry, control of illicit crops, etc. The expulsion of thousands of peasant farmers from their lands brought about a land recomposition and restructuring. Large estates have grown, and there are fewer and fewer estate owners. The geographic expansion of the conflict, the increase and versatility of violent actions, as well as constant human rights violations perpetrated with quasi-total impunity have increased forced displacements during these past years.

Shantytowns in big cities are usually the final destination of the displaced, as they are believed to guarantee anonymity, security, and the illusion of an alternative lifestyle. However, security threats can go on even after displacement takes place. Therefore, these people often try to maintain anonymity and conceal their conditions. Consequently, many refuse to contact public institutions and never obtain access to government programs. Displaced people are also stigmatized. They are identified with a party in the conflict, mainly the guerrillas, and are believed "to have done some harm." They are seen as a potential source of conflict and violence, and as a burden upon the social services system. Municipalities and institutions are not willing to receive displaced people or assist them.

Once the emergency stage is over, displaced people are included in the contingent of people known in Colombia as "the living poor." Upon being identified as poor (and not displaced), they can only benefit from social policies that target vulnerable groups. Government policies are assistance-oriented; do not take into consideration the causes of forced displacement or human rights violations, and do not include compensation, protection, or prevention. Although some progress has been made concerning the formulation of laws and regulations, there is still a long way to go for them to be applied effectively. As new policies and measures lack coordination and resources, their implementation depends wholly on international funds.

Access to the government system is complex and restrictive. The lack of sufficient information regarding the steps to take and bureaucratic obstacles hinder many displaced people from requesting help. Registration can take anywhere from one or two months to years. To gain access to government services, a displaced person is required to report the party to blame for the displacement, which can jeopardize a person's security. Due to leaks in official institutions, some people have been chased, arrested, and even killed for reporting such information.

It can be said that the state has no political will: each new government addresses the problem from scratch, and the institutions in charge of this matter are constantly changing, creating delays. Institutions at the departmental and municipal levels are overwhelmed by the magnitude of the problem and have no resources, and sometimes no will, to take the necessary measures. The state does not acknowledge displacement as a human rights violation; therefore, the displaced must negotiate access to their rights, often through protests and lobbies. Displacement and the economic policies to which it is linked are causing the exclusion of many social groups, as well as social disruption that reaches dramatic levels in many areas in the country. Some studies show that the high incidence of psychosocial disorders is a consequence of traumatic experiences, and that psychosocial assistance is extremely important. The trauma caused by displacement, especially in children—who comprise half of the displaced population—has yet to be assessed thoroughly.

There is a lack of awareness about the situation and rights of the displaced. The available information and analysis do not reach the public, which relies on television—a media outlet that is highly prejudiced against the displaced—as its main source of information. Fernando Medellín, the director of the Social Solidarity Network, admits this fact in the following text:

> News telecasts from the main television stations in Bogotá say
> that "something" happened in Tulúa. And in Tulúa people
> say "something" happened in Monteloro. That "something"

is the murder of civilians, which has also meant a threat for the inhabitants totally alien to the conflict, causing them to flee to the main town in the municipality. News is given in a casual, hasty manner, and people then put their imaginations to work: "Somebody must have owed something and somebody paid for this".... By means of the news conveyed by the media, people have come to believe that forced displacement due to violence is not linked to natural resources—to coal or gold mine exploitations or oil—or to the building of large hydroelectric projects, or even to the announcement of possible investments in areas usually inhabited by poor people, who have some land but who are not landowners.[53]

The Colombian government defines displacement as an effect of the conflict and of the fighting among irregular groups and describes itself as just another victim, unable to put an end to it. But it is neither a circumstantial nor a short-term problem for that matter, and addressing it through specific, assistance-oriented responses in a fragmented, partial way will not have a long-lasting impact on the dynamic that drives population movements.

Forced displacement in Colombia is not included in peace-negotiation agendas or congressional debates. It does not receive the public attention that abductions and disappearances get. Those displaced "by violence" are a group forsaken by the system, though they are not the only ones: small farmers who cultivate illicit crops and are compared to drug traffickers, those who are expelled from their lands under the pressure exerted by the economic system, and those excluded from the labor market are all forgotten populations.

With respect to international involvement, classifying the long and complex Colombian conflict as a problem of terrorism and drug trafficking may serve to justify policies of force, but it does not serve to resolve Colombia's problems, and it will not lead to an end of the war. The causes of this war are rooted in the problems of political and economic exclusion, inequality in land ownership, patrimonial control of the state by the elite, and a lack of real democratic and legitimate institutions, among other factors. Winning the war does not seem to be within the reach of any of the groups, but while this policy remains in effect, only more death and suffering can be expected for the population. It is urgent that the task of reinforcing some truly democratic institutions be undertaken, as well as strengthening the judicial system and respect for human rights, without forgetting the need to eliminate social inequalities and political exclusion and to create the conditions for development in peace. Colombian society, as rich and diverse as it is, has a lot to contribute to this process and, therefore, also to peace building in Colombia, a peace that can not only mean the absence of war, but a renewed legitimization of the state, the protection and guarantee of rights to the society, and the strengthening of human security. In sum, a basic reformation of civil society and the state.

1   Jorge Rojas and Marco Romero, "Conflicto armado y desplazamiento forzado interno en Colombia," in *Esta guerra no es nuestra: Niños y desplazamiento forzado en Colombia* (Bogotá: CODHES-UNICEF, 2000).

2   Gabriel García Márquez, *Cien años de soledad* (Barcelona: Círculo de Lectores, 1989), 90.

3   Liliana Obregón and Maria Stavropoulou, "In Search of Hope: The Plight of Displaced Colombians," in *The Forsaken People: Case Studies of the Internally Displaced*, R. Cohen and F. Deng, eds. (Washington, D.C.: Brookings Institution Press, 1998).

4   Marbel Sandoval, "Desplazados: una historia sin contar," *Universitas Humanística*, no. 47, January–June 1999, 33–44.

5   Alfredo Molano, "El Plan Colombia: Versiones," unpublished document, September 8, 2000.

6   Jaime Zuluaga Nieto, "Antecedentes y tendencias del desplazamiento forzoso en Colombia," in *El desplazamiento por la violencia en Colombia: experiencias, análisis y posibles estrategias de atención en el Departamento de Antioquia: memorias del Foro Internacional "Desplazados Internos en Antioquia," Medellín, 27–28 de julio de 1998,* Carlos Tassara, Dalia María Jimenez Castrillón, Luigi Grando, and Yolanda Zuluaga Torres, eds. (Medellín, Colombia: CISP, Comitato internazionale per lo sviluppo dei popoli; ACNUR; Pastoral Social, Arquidiócesis de Medellín, 1999).

7   Darío Fajardo, "Bases para una política de asentamientos humanos, prevención de los desplazamientos forzados y acceso a la tierra para los desplazados," Final Assessment Report for the Joint Technical Unit, UNHCR-RSS Bogotá, November 12, 2000, unpublished document.

8   National Indigenous Organization in Colombia (ONIC), *Para retornar ... a la vida, Memorias del Encuentro Nacional de Desplazados,* report, Bogotá, February 23–25, 2000.

9   Juan de Dios Mosquera, *Las comunidades negras de Colombia hacia el siglo XXI* (Bogotá: Docentes Editores, 2000).

10 Interview with José Domingo Caldón, CRIC vice president, Bogotá, July 13, 2001.

11 "First, violence does not correlate with the poorest areas of the country. Rather, violence is correlated with areas featuring a high concentration of land and wealth. In fact, Colombia has one of the greatest disparities of wealth and land concentration of any country—a trend that has worsened in the past fifteen years. Land concentration in contemporary Colombia resembles patterns of nineteenth century Latin American ownership, as the country never underwent a major land reform." *The Economics of War: The Intersection of Need, Creed and Greed,* conference report, Woodrow Wilson International Center, September 10, 2001.

12 Rojas and Romero, "Conflicto armado y desplazamiento."

13 Fernando Medellín and Ulises Rinaudo, "Los desafíos de la política de reasentamiento de población desplazada por la violencia," in *Reasentamiento en Colombia,* William Partridge, ed. (Bogotá, World Bank, 2000).

14 Lauchlin Currie, *Desarrollo económico acelerado* (Mexico DF: Fondo de Cultura Económica, 1968).

15 Pastoral Social, *RUT Informa,* no. 2, April–June 1999, Bogotá, 11.

16 "Campesinos, una especie en vías de extinción," *El Tiempo,* August 5, 2001.

17 Tamara Osorio, et al., "Estados frágiles, ruptura de equilibrios y exclusión," *Cuadernos para el debate,* no. 1, Médicos Sin Fronteras—Spain, Barcelona, 2000.

18 See, for example, Mary Kaldor, *New and Old Wars: Organized Violence in a Global Era* (Stanford, California: Stanford University Press, 1999); Mabel González Bustelo, "Conflictos olvidados," in *Conflictos en la sociedad globalizada: preguntas y respuestas. Nuevas dimensiones a la luz de la guerra en Irak* (to be published by UCLM in 2004); and the CIP Yearbooks of the past few years.

19 Juan Gabriel Tokatlián and José Luis Ramírez, eds., *La violencia de las armas en*

Colombia (Bogotá: Fundación Alejandro Ángel Escobar-Tercer Mundo, 1995).

20 Nazih Richani, "The Political Economy of Violence: The War System in Colombia," *Journal of Inter-American Studies and World Affairs*, vol. 39, no. 2, 37–82.

21 Except when specified, all data in this chapter comes from official sources: Departamento Nacional de Planeación—Unidad de Desarrollo Social—División de Indicadores y Orientación del Gasto Social; Departamento Administrativo Nacional de Estadística and Sistema de Indicadores Sociodemográficos. Excerpts from Libardo Sarmiento Anzola, "Plan Colombia, conflicto e intervención," *Nueva Sociedad*, no. 172, March–April 2001, Caracas; and Libardo Sarmiento Anzola, "El Plan Colombia y la economía política de la guerra," unpublished document.

22 Magda Rivera, "A diez años de la apertura: Un balance diferente," published in CINEP magazine *Cien Días*, available online at http://www.cinep.org.co.

23 Informe de Desarrollo Humano 2003, *El conflicto, callejón con salida* (Bogotá: UNPD, 2003).

24 Francis Deng, "Report of the Representative of the Secretary-General on internally displaced persons submitted in accordance with Commission resolution 1999/47. Addendum: Profiles in displacement; Follow-up mission to Colombia," UN Commission on Human Rights, fifty-fifth session, document no. E/CN.4/2000/83/Add.1, January 11, 2000.

25 This section is based on Mabel González Bustelo, "Colombia, de la guerra antidrogas a la guerra contra el terrorismo," in *Colombia. La guerra que no para*, Mabel González Bustelo and José Aristizábal García, eds. (Cordoba: Ayuntamiento de Córdoba-IECAH-INET, 2004).

26 Editorial, "Origen, objetivos y efectos del ALCA," *Alternativas Sur*, vol. 2, no. 1, 2003, 11.

27 Alfredo Molano, "El Plan Colombia y el conflicto armado," *América Latina en Movimiento* (ALAINET), October 10, 2000.

28 Mabel González Bustelo, "Drogas, narcotráfico y guerra en Colombia," in *Bienes comunes en conflicto*, Ricardo Aguilar, ed. (Madrid: La Casa Encendida, 2003).

29 Alfredo Molano, "El Plan Colombia y el conflicto armado."

30 Mabel González Bustelo, "Drogas, narcotráfico y guerra."

31 Transnational Institute, "Fumigaciones y conflicto en Colombia: Al calor del debate," *Drogas y conflicto. Documentos de debate*, no. 2, September 2001.

32 There are no scientific studies on the impact of this herbicide on human health and the environment under the conditions experienced in Colombia: high concentrations of the dosages and wide-scale fumigations. Various organizations (indigenous, civil society, etc.) and even governmental institutions such as the public defender's and governors' offices have requested on repeated occasions that the fumigations be stopped until their innocuousness is proven; however, the argument that the fumigations have yet to be proven to cause harmful effects is usually used against these requests.

33 Juan Tokatlián, *Globalización, narcotráfico y violencia* (Bogotá: Norma Editores, 2000).

34 "'Currently, there are 69,000 hectares of the leaf,'" *El Tiempo,* September 19, 2003.

35 United States, Department of State, International Narcotics Control Strategy Report, Washington, D.C., March 2003, available online at http://www.state.gov/g/inl/rls/nrcrpt/.

36 Rita Cruz, "Luchas sociales en América Latina," *Papeles de cuestiones internacionales,* no. 84, winter 2003–04.

37 Speech made by Álvaro Uribe before the Inter-American Court of Human Rights, cited by CODHES, 2003.

38 CODHES, 2003.

39 United States Institute of Peace, "U.S. Involvement Deepens as Armed Conflict Escalates in Colombia," May 21, 2003, available online at http://www.usip.org.

40 Some of these restrictions on public freedoms and the criminalization of dissidence have a surprising parallelism to measures applied in the United States, as per the USA PATRIOT Act, which have been justified by the war against terrorism.

41 Gabriel Marcella, "The United States and Colombia: The Journey from Ambiguity to Strategic Clarity," The Dante B. Fascell North-South Center, *Working Paper Series,* no. 13, March 2003.

42 Eduardo Pizarro and Ana María Bejarano, "Colombia. ¿Guerra civil, contra la sociedad, guerra ambigua o antiterrorista?" *América Latina: Democracia, neoliberalismo, populismo; La Vanguardia Dossier,* no. 4, January–March 2003.

43 "Walters Links Drugs to Terrorism," *Washington Times,* October 11, 2003.

44 Center for International Policy, "The United States and Colombia, 2003: A Look at the Numbers," October 28, 2003, available online at http://www.ciponline.org/colombia/031028stat.htm.

45 See Center for International Policy, "U.S. Aid to Colombia Since 1997: Summary Tables."

46 Ingrid Vaicius and Adam Isacson, "The War on Drugs Meets the War on Terror," *CIP International Policy Report,* February 2003.

47 Carolina María Rudas, "Paradojas y contradicciones en Colombia: una mirada al año 2003," in *Anuario CIP 2004: Escenarios de conflicto: Irak y el desorden mundial,* Manuela Mesa and Mabel González Bustelo, eds. (Barcelona: Icaria, 2004).

48 Plataforma Colombiana de Derechos Humanos, *El Embrujo autoritario: Primer año del Gobierno de Álvaro Uribe Velez,* Bogotá, September 2003.

49 Quoted in Garry Leech, "Record Numbers 'Disappeared' in Colombia's 'Dirty War,'" *The New Standard,* February 2, 2004.

50 CODHES, *Guerra y confinamiento. ¿Desplazados sin salida?,* CODHES-Informa, vol. 7, no. 46, December 10, 2003. CODHES attributes the trend to various factors that

come from the restructuring of the conflict, the strategic appropriation of the territory, and the political economy of the war.

51 Ibid.

52 CODHES, 2003.

53 Medellín and Rinaudo, "Los desafíos de la política de reasentamiento de la población desplazada por la violencia."

Glossary

Acronyms

AFRODES Association of Afro-Colombian Displaced (*Asociación de Afrocolombianos Desplazados*)

ANUC National Farmers' Association (*Asociación Nacional de Usuarios Campesinos*)

ARS Subsidized Health Plan (*Administradoras del Régimen Subsidiado*)

ASOAGROMISBOL Southern Bolívar Farmers' and Miners' Association (*Asociación de Agricultores y Mineros del Sur de Bolívar*)

AUC United Self-Defense Forces of Colombia (*Autodefensas Unidas de Colombia*)

CCJ Colombian Commission of Jurists (*Comisión Colombiana de Juristas*)

CND National Coordinator of the Displaced (*Coordinadora Nacional de Desplazados*)

CODHES Consultancy on Human Rights and Displacement (*Consultoría para los Derechos Humanos y El Desplazamiento*)

CONPES National Council of Economic and Social Policy (*Consejo Nacional de Política Económica y Social*)

CRIC Cauca's Regional Indigenous Council (*Consejo Regional Indígena del Cauca*)

DAS Administrative Department for Security (*Departamento Administrativo de Seguridad*)

DIAL Interagency Dialogue (*Diálogo Interagencial*)

DNP National Planning Department (*Departamento Nacional de Planeación*)

ECHO European Community Humanitarian Office

ELN National Liberation Army (*Ejército de Liberación Nacional*)

EPL People's Liberation Party (*Ejército Popular de Liberación*)

EPS Health Care Centers (*Entidades Promotoras de Salud*)

241

EZLN National Liberation Zapatista Army *(Ejército Zapatista de Liberación Nacional)*

FAO Food and Agriculture Organization of the United Nations

FARC–EP Revolutionary Armed Forces of Colombia *Fuerzas Armadas Revolucionarias de Colombia–Ejército del Pueblo*

FOSYGA Solidarity and Guarantee Fund *(Fondo de Solidaridad y Garantía)*

FTAA Free Trade Area of the Americas

GAD Support Group of Displaced Populations *(Grupo de Apoyo a Desplazados)*

GNP Gross National Product

GTD Thematic Group on Displacement *(Grupo Temático de Desplazamiento)*

ICRC International Committee of the Red Cross

IHL International Humanitarian Law

IMF International Monetary Fund

INCORA Colombian Agrarian Reform Institute *(Instituto Colombiano de Reforma Agraria)*

IOM International Organization for Migration

IPS Health Institution *(Institución Prestadora de Salud)*

OCHA United Nations Office for the Coordination of Humanitarian Affairs

OEA Organization of American States *(Organización de Estados Americanos)*

ONIC Colombian National Indigenous Organization *(Organización Nacional Indígena de Colombia)*

PAHO Pan-American Health Organization

RSS Social Solidarity Network *(Red de Solidaridad Social)*

SEFC Contrasting Sources Information System *(Sistema de Estimación por Fuentes Contrastadas)*

SISDES Information System on Internal Displacement *(Sistema de Información sobre Desplazamiento Interno)*

SNAIPD Comprehensive Assistance to Displaced People National System *(Sistema Nacional de Atención Integral a Población Desplazada)*

UAO Assistance and Orientation Units *(Unidad de Atención y Orientación)*

UNICEF United Nation Children's Fund

UNDP United Nations Development Program

UNHCHR United Nations High Commissioner for Human Rights

UNHCR United Nations High Commissioner for Refugees

UP Patriotic Union *(Unión Patriótica)*

WB World Bank

WFP World Food Program

Glossary

agua de panela § drink made with raw brown sugar, hot water, and lemon

aguardiente § alcohol made from distilled sugar cane and anise

ají § hot peppers; spicy sauce made with ajies, green onions, cilantro, tomatoes, and salt

amapola § opium poppy from which opium gum is extracted and heroin is made

antioqueños § people from Antioquia province

Apartadó § town in northwest Antioquia

arepa § small corn cake made with corn meal, water, salt, and oil

arriero § mule driver

autodefensas § self-defense forces; what the paramilitaries call themselves

bambucos § popular Colombian dance, descended from Africa

barbudos § catfish

Barranca § Barrancabermeja

basuco § mix of cocaine and heroin, or a cigarette laced with cocaine, marijuana, and other substances

biche § alcohol made from fermented sugar cane

Boca de Cajambre § mouth of the Cajambre River

boyaco § somone from the department (regional governing entity) of Boyacá, near Bogotá

buseta § small passenger bus

cabildo § council that groups together a community's traditional authorities

campesino § farmworker or peasant

(la) catira § woman with reddish, blond hair and greenish eyes; usually said of someone whose parents are mixed race, white and black

cativo § tropical hardwood native to Central and South American rain forests

cédula § identification card

chachajo § tree whose wood is used in construction

chicha § alcohol made from fermented corn or fruit

chicharrón § pork rind

chontaduro § plum-sized fruit

chulavita § paramilitary death squads set up by the Conservative Party in the late 1940s, named for the town from which many of them were recruited

colono § settler, colonist

cordillera § Andes mountains

crónica § story, history, or testimony

curubo § tree from which the curuba (banana passionfruit) comes

DAS § Colombian civilian police

DAS/F2 § Colombian police intelligence

descuajado § liquified, transformed from a solid into a liquid form; used in text to describe a baby whose internal organs were born outside of his body

fique § textile plant; its fibers are used to make rope

fraylejon(es) § a high-desert plant with a tall stock and long leaves

gamin(es) § street children

granadilla § passion fruit

guarapo § alcohol made from fermented sugar cane

guatin(es) § rodent relative of Guinea pig, lives in Central and South American forests

guatinaja § see *guatin(es)*

indigo § perennial and leguminous tree; the dark blue color dough obtained for macerating the stems and leaves of this tree

junta § governing council

La Mano Negra § "Black Hand" death squad

La Mona § woman's nickname

llanero § person who lives or works in the plains region

llano § plain; a large expanse of flat land, often used for raising lifestock

matón § killer

mellizo(a) § twin

Moya de los Chulos § a whirlpool in the river where vultures congregate

muchachos § "guys"; slang for guerrillas

natilla § popular Christmas custard made with milk, sugar, cornstarch, cinnamon and coconut

Nechí § town in northeast Antioquia

negrola § common Latin American description of a person of African descent; also used colloquially as a term of endearment, like "honey" or "sweetie"

Organización Campesina del Bajo Cauca § organization for peasants from the lower Cauca River region

paisa § person from the Medillin/ Antioquia region; also the Spanish dialect of this region

panela § raw brown sugar

paracos § paramilitaries

páramo § high-altitude grassland wilderness

pipire § regional name for chontaduro

pisingo § wild duck

quinine § quinine tree bark which contains quinine with medicinal properties

sancocho (de gallina) § popular soup containing chicken, corn, potato, yucca, and plantain

sapos § snitches, informants

sicarios § hired killers

tejo § traditional game in which players throw heavy iron discs (tejos) at triangle-shaped blasting caps embedded in mounds of hard earth or mud

tinto § black coffee

Tirofijo § "Sureshot"—nickname of Pedro Antonio Marín, legendary FARC guerrilla founder and leader

vacaloca § bonfire lit during street parties held in towns or neighborhoods during the December holidays

valluno § person from Cali and surrounding areas; also the Spanish dialect of this region

yonson § motorboat

Resources on Colombia
on the World Wide Web

Media

Colombia

Cambio: http://www.cambio.com.co

El Colombiano: http://www.elcolombiano.terra.com.co

El Espectador: http://www.elespectador.com

El Tiempo: http://eltiempo.terra.com.co

Radio Caracol: http://caracol.com.co

RCN: http://www.rcnradio.com.co

Semana: http://semana.terra.com.co

International

Latin American Information Agency: http://www.alainet.org

International Press Service: http://www.ips.org/latam.shtml

BBC: http://news.bbc.co.uk

CNN: http://www.cnn.com

El Mundo (Spain): http://www.elmundo.es

El País (Spain): http://www.elpais.es

Financial Times: http://www.ft.com

International Herald Tribune: http://www.iht.com

The Economist: http://www.economist.com

The Guardian: http://www.guardian.co.uk

The New York Times: http://www.nytimes.com

The Washington Post: http://www.washingtonpost.com

Nongovernmental organizations and independent media (in alphabetical order)

Campaign for Labor Rights:
http://www.campaignforlaborrights.org

Centre for International Policy: http://www.ciponline.org/
colombia

CINEP (Centro de Investigación y Educación Popular):
http://www.cinep.org.co

Centro de Medios Independientes Colombia:
http://colombia.indymedia.org

**Consultoría para los Derechos Humanos y El Desplazamiento
(CODHES):** http://www.codhes.org.co

Colombia Action Network:
http://www.colombiaactionnetwork.org

Colombia Human Rights Network: http://www.colhrnet.igc.org

Colombia Journal: http://www.colombiajournal.org

Colombia Support Network: http://www.colombiasupport.net

Colombia Times: http://www.colombiatimes.com

Comisión Interamericana de Derechos Humanos:
http://www.cidh.org

Equipo Nizkor: http://www.derechos.org/nizkor/colombia

Global IDP Project: http://www.idpproject.org

Human Rights Watch: http://www.hrw.org/campaigns/colombia

Instituto Interamericano de Derechos Humanos:
http://www.iidh.ed.cr

Instituto Latinoamericano de Servicios Legales Alternativos: http://www.ilsa.org.co

Killer Coke Campaign: http://www.killercoke.org

Latin America Information Network (LANIC): http://lanic.utexas.edu/la/colombia

Latin America Watch: http://www.zmag.org/LAM/index

Naciones Unidas (Coordinación Humanitaria): http://www.reliefweb.int

National Secretariat of Pastoral Social (SNPS)–Cáritas Colombiana: http://www.pastoralsocialcolombia.org

North American Congress on Latin American (NACLA) *Report on the Americas*: http://www.nacla.org

Norway Refugee Council: http://www.nrc.no

Oneworld América Latina: http://amlat.oneworld.net

Organización Panamericana de la Salud: http://www.col.ops-oms.org

Paz Colombia: http://www.galeon.com/pazcolombia

Planeta Paz: http://www.planetapaz.org

Refugee Studies Centre: http://www.rsc.ox.ac.uk

Resource Center of the Americas: http://www.americas.org/colombia

Sindicato Nacional de Trabajadores de la Industria de Alimentos (National Union of Food Industry Workers) http://www.sinaltrainal.org

Transnational Institute (programa "drogas y democracia"): http://www.tni.org/drugs

UN High Commission on Human Rights (Colombia): http://www.hchr.org.co

UN High Commission on Human Rights (International): http://www.ohchr.org/english

United States Committee for Refugees (USCR): http://www.refugees.org

United States Institute of Peace:
http://www.usip.org/library/regions/colombia

Washington Office on Latin America: http://www.wola.org

Official sources and armed actors in Colombia and the U.S.

Autodefensas Unidas de Colombia: http://www.colombialibre.org

Defensoría del Pueblo: http://www.defensoria.org.co

Departamento Nacional de Planeación: http://www.dnp.gov.co

Ejército de Liberación Nacional: http://www.eln-voces.com

Fuerzas Armadas Revolucionarias de Colombia (FARC):
http://www.farcep.org

Presidencia de la República: http://www.presidencia.gov.co

Red de Solidaridad Social: http://www.red.gov.co

Ministerio de Defensa: http://www.mindefensa.gov.co

U.S. Embassies and Consulates: http://usembassy.state.gov

U.S. Library of Congress: http://www.loc.gov

U.S. Department of State: http://www.state.gov/p/wha/ci/co

Contributors

Aviva Chomsky is Professor of Latin American History and Coordinator of Latin American, Latino, and Caribbean Studies at Salem State College in Massachusetts. Her books include *West Indian Workers and the United Fruit Company in Costa Rica, 1870–1940* (1996), *Identity and Struggle at the Margins of the Nation-State: Central America and the Hispanic Caribbean* (coedited with Aldo Lauria-Santiago, 1998), and *The Cuba Reader: History, Culture, Politics* (coedited with Barry Carr and Pamela Smorkaloff, 2003). She has been active for two decades in the Central America, Cuba, and Colombia solidarity movements.

Daniel Bland is a Canadian journalist and documentary filmmaker. He lived in Colombia during most of the 1990s, working as a writer and human rights researcher.

Mabel González Bustelo is a journalist and analyst at the Centro de la Investigación para la Paz (CIP, Peace Research Center) in Madrid, Spain. She is coeditor of the CIP's Yearbook and has published articles and essays on international issues and trends. She has worked in Colombia, conducting research on forced displacement of the civil population, and also in Angola on the role of the media and civil society in the reconstruction process. González Bustelo has taught university courses on international relations, armed conflicts, and humanitarian action. Currently, the CIP is engaged in a project, "The Role of the European Union in the Peace Process in Colombia," which will produce research and publications through 2006. For more information, visit the CIP's Web page at www.ciponline.org/colombia. To contact the author, e-mail mabelgonzalez@teleline.es.

Lance Selfa is an editor of and contributor to the *International Socialist Review*. He edited *The Struggle for Palestine* (Haymarket, 2002). He is a member of the National Writers Union.

ABOUT HAYMARKET BOOKS

Haymarket Books is a non-profit, progressive book distributor and publisher, a project of the Center for Economic Research and Social Change.

We believe that activists need to take ideas, history and politics into the many struggles for social justice today. Learning the lessons of past victories, as well as defeats, can arm a new generation of fighters for a better world. As Karl Marx said, "The philosophers have merely interpreted the world; the point however is to change it."

We take inspiration and courage from our namesakes, the Haymarket Martyrs, who gave their lives fighting for a better world. Their struggle for the eight-hour day in 1886, which gave us May Day, the international workers' holiday, reminds workers around the world that ordinary people can organize and struggle for their own liberation. These struggles continue today in every corner of the globe—struggles against oppression, exploitation, hunger and poverty.

It was August Spies, one of the Martyrs who was targeted for being an immigrant and an anarchist, who predicted the battles being fought to this day. "If you think that by hanging us you can stamp out the labor movement," Spies told the judge, "then hang us. Here you will tread upon a spark, but here, and there, and behind you, and in front of you, and everywhere, the flames will blaze up. It is a subterranean fire. You cannot put it out. The ground is on fire upon which you stand."

Visit our online bookstore at www.haymarketbooks.org.

We could not succeed in our publishing efforts without the generous financial support of our readers. Many people contribute to our project through the Haymarket Sustainers program, where donors receive free books in return for their monetary support. If you would like to be a part of this program, please contact us at info@haymarketbooks.org.

ALSO FROM HAYMARKET BOOKS

WHAT'S MY NAME, FOOL? SPORTS AND RESISTANCE IN THE UNITED STATES

Dave Zirin   1 931859 20 5   July 2005

Edgeofsports.com sportswriter Dave Zirin provdes a no-holds-barred commentary on the personalities and politics of American sports.

"Zirin is America's best sportswriter."—Lee Ballinger, *Rock and Rap Confidential*

WOMEN AND SOCIALISM

Sharon Smith   1 931859 11 6   May 2005

The fight for women's liberation is urgent—and must be linked to winning broader social change.

A PEOPLE'S HISTORY OF IRAQ: THE IRAQI COMMUNIST PARTY, WORKERS' MOVEMENTS, AND THE LEFT 1924–2004

Ilario Salucci   1 931859 14 0   April 2005

Iraqis have a long tradition of fighting against foreign and domestic tyranny. Here is their story.

THE WORLD SOCIAL FORUM: STRATEGIES OF RESISTANCE

José Corrêa Leite   1 931859 15 9   April 2005

The inside story of how the worldwide movement against corporate globalization has become such a force.

YOUR MONEY OR YOUR LIFE (3rd edition)

Eric Toussaint   1 931859 18 3   June 2005

Globalization brings growth? Think again. Debt—engineered by the IMF and World Bank—sucks countries dry.

LITERATURE AND REVOLUTION

Leon Trotsky   1 931859 21 3   May 2005

A new, annotated edition of Leon Trotsky's classic study of the relationship of politics and art.

THE THEORY OF REVOLUTION IN THE YOUNG MARX

Michael Löwy   1 931859 19 1   June 2005

The ideas of Marx's early writings come alive in this important examination of their lasting relevance.

THE STRUGGLE FOR PALESTINE

Lance Selfa, Ed.   1 931859 00 0   2002

In this important collection of essays, leading international solidarity activists offer insight into the ongoing struggle for Palestinian freedom and for justice in the Middle East.

THE FORGING OF THE AMERICAN EMPIRE

Sidney Lens   0 745321 00 3   2002

This is the story of a nation—the United States—that has conducted more than 160 wars and other military ventures while insisting that it loves peace. In the process, the U.S. has forged a world empire while maintaining its innocence of imperialistic designs. Includes a new introduction by Howard Zinn.

AMERICAN SOCIALIST MOVEMENT: 1897-1912

Ira Kipnis   1 931859 12 4   2004

The American Socialist Party, at the height of its power, had more than 150,000 members and won almost a million votes for its presidential candidate. Few books have more to offer to the student of the movement than this one.

THE CASE FOR SOCIALISM

Alan Maass   1 931859 09 4   2004

"[Maass'] book charts a game plan for realistic radicals, who haven't given up hope for making revolutionary changes in a society that finds itself in the grip of a remorseless political entropy. Take cheer: History isn't over. In fact, it's hardly even begun for us. Read Maass. Then go out and make some."

—Jeffrey St. Clair, coeditor of *CounterPunch*

Order these titles and more online at www.haymarketbooks.org
or call 773-583-7884.

Haymarket Books is distributed to bookstores by Consortium Book Sales
and Distribution, www.cbsd.com.